The MacGeough Bonds of The Argory

Maynooth Studies in Local History

SERIES EDITOR Raymond Gillespie

This is one of six short books published in the Maynooth Studies in Local History series in 2005. Like their predecessors they are, in the main, drawn from theses presented for the MA course in local history at NUI Maynooth. Also, like their predecessors, they range widely over the local experience in the Irish past. That local experience is presented in the context of the complex social and political world of which it is part, from the great houses of Armagh to the rural housing of Leitrim and from the property developers of eighteenth-century Dublin to those who rioted on the streets of the capital. The local experience cannot be a simple chronicling of events relating to an area within administrative or geographically-determined boundaries since understanding the local world presents much more complex challenges for the historian. It is an investigation of the socially diverse worlds of poor and rich. It explores the lives of those who joined the British army in the First World War as well as those who, on principle, chose not to do so. Reconstructing such diverse local worlds relies on understanding what the people of the different communities that made up the localities of Ireland had in common and what drove them apart. Understanding the assumptions, often unspoken, around which these local societies operated is the key to recreating the world of the Irish past and gaining insight into how the people who inhabited those worlds lived their daily lives. As such, studies such as those presented in these short books, together with their predecessors, are at the forefront of Irish historical research and represent some of the most innovative and exciting work being undertaken in Irish history today. They also provide models that others can follow and adapt in their own studies of the Irish past. In such ways can we better understand the regional diversity of Ireland and the social and cultural basis of that diversity. If these books also convey something of the vibrancy and excitement of the world of Irish local history today they will have achieved at least some of their purpose.

Maynooth Studies in Local History: Number 62

The MacGeough Bonds of The Argory

An Ulster gentry family, 1880–1950

Olwen Purdue

FOUR COURTS PRESS

Set in 10pt on 12pt Bembo by
Carrigboy Typesetting Services, County Cork for
FOUR COURTS PRESS LTD
7 Malpas Street, Dublin 8, Ireland
e-mail: info@four-courts-press.ie
http://www.four-courts-press.ie
and in North America for
FOUR COURTS PRESS
c/o ISBS, 920 N.E. 58th Avenue, Suite 300, Portland, OR 97213.

ISBN 1–85182–894–X

Printed in Ireland by
ßetaprint Ltd, Dublin

Contents

Preface

In my research for this work I was helped by a wide number of people to whom I would like to express my gratitude. First of all, I am indebted to Mrs Isobel Wright, Mr Bond's one-time housekeeper and close friend, whose knowledge and enthusiasm for the family's history initially inspired me to embark on this study. I am also grateful to Derek Forshaw and the staff at The Argory who facilitated me in every way they could and always made me feel most welcome.

My thanks are due to all at the Public Record Office of Northern Ireland: my work was made so much easier by their friendliness and courteousness as well as by the efficiency with which they dealt with my requests. I would also like to thank my supervisor, Brian Walker, and the staff at the Institute of Irish Studies for all their help and advice.

Finally, and most importantly, I owe a deep debt of gratitude to my family without whose unfailing support and understanding this work could never have been completed.

Introduction

Travelling through the Co. Armagh countryside near its border with Tyrone, the roads wind their way round the drumlins that give this part of the country its distinctive character. The farming land is generally good, but fields are small and sometimes, on the lower land, tend to be boggy. This is apple country, a fact that cannot escape any visitor to the area as field after field is given over to the cultivation of rows of fruit trees. Occasionally the landscape changes; open country is replaced with a dense concentration of deciduous trees, fences give way to high stone walls, entrances are guarded by imposing gatelodges. One gets the impression that something is being protected, hidden from view, shielded from its surroundings. Often the shrubberies are too dense or the distance too great to afford a view of what lies beyond. Sometimes, however, a gap in the trees might offer an alluring glimpse of the structure that lies at the heart of this great enclosure, one of the mansions that were the country homes of the ruling elite – Ireland's 'big houses'.

Today, however, the curious passer-by who is prompted to take a closer look at the homes of Ireland's aristocracy is often met with disappointment. More careful inspection reveals that once high walls are crumbling away and that the trees, laurels and rhododendrons, now running riot in a wilderness, shield from public gaze the shame of desolation and destruction. For now, 150 years after the ascendancy was at its height, many of the great houses that represented its power and prestige have been abandoned, lie in ruins or have completely disappeared. Many of the big houses of Armagh and south Tyrone have shared this fate. Those families that formed the social circle of gentry in this area, that met for tea and tennis, that hunted and shot and dined together are now largely a part of history, distant memories for the local population. Of their grand homes there is, in some cases, no hint that they ever existed. Others remain in varying states of decay; a few have remained intact, but as empty buildings rather than the family homes they were intended to be.

These houses and their demesnes, together the physical manifestation of the Anglo-Irish ascendancy, have long been a familiar feature of the Irish countryside, not least in this area close to the ancient ecclesiastical city of Armagh. Once the mansions lay at the very heart of rural society, inhabited by that small number of families who not only owned the land but whose influence and authority extended to all aspects of rural life. The late eighteenth and early nineteenth centuries in particular had witnessed a tremendous increase in the amount of building going on in the countryside as well as in the towns. Nobles, peers and country gentlemen, confident in their continuing role as leaders of Irish society, were actively engaged in building or rebuilding mansions on their estates. They desired houses that would reflect their status and power; they also desired houses that would be a lasting tribute to their refinement and taste. In many cases the latter influence led to extensive redesigning or replacing of houses as the classical lines of Georgian Ireland gave way to the more flamboyant and romantic taste of the Victorian era.

In Ulster, as throughout Ireland, landlords were busy planning and build-ing mansions to be enjoyed not only by themselves but by the generations they believed would follow them. Work was begun on Baron's Court, country seat of the Abercorns, in around 1780. Ten years later Lord Belmore began what Mark Bence-Jones has described as 'the most palatial house in Ireland.'[1] Costing somewhere in the region of £90,000, a staggering figure in eighteenth-century terms, Castle Coole was built out of Portland stone, with each piece having to be brought from the Isle of Wight by boat, barge and bullock cart. In the east of the province, outside the town of Bangor, Lord Dufferin had begun work on Clandeboye in around 1820, while not far away work was soon to start on Lord Londonderry's Mount Stewart. Landlords in the Armagh area were not left behind in the general building frenzy of the period. Around the time of his marriage in 1810 Sir James Stronge completely transformed the late-seventeenth-century house on his estate at Tynan, adding towers, battlements and pinnacles in true Tudor-Gothic style. In keeping with its romantic appearance the property was renamed Tynan Abbey, described in 1835 by Lieutenant C. Bailey of the Ordnance Survey as 'a remarkable handsome building' with a demesne that was 'extensive and well-planted'.[2] Lord Lurgan also favoured this romantic Tudor-revival style of architecture for his new mansion, Brownlow House, begun in 1838. Designed by the Edinburgh architect W.H. Playfair, this house is described by Brett as 'the grandest architectural set-piece in the county'.[3]

This strong influence of romanticism was also evident in two other dramatic big houses built during the 1830s. The duke of Manchester's Tanderagee Castle, with its oriels, archways and turrets, perched high on the edge of a ravine and surrounded by dense woods, would not have been out of place in a story book populated with princesses and ogres. Work began on the castle in 1830 and by 1837 it was ready for habitation,[4] something which must have been discouraging for the duke's neighbour, the earl of Gosford whose massive Norman-revival fortress, Gosford Castle, was taking much longer to complete. Gosford had commissioned the London architect, William Hopper, and building work had commenced in 1819. By 1837, as the finishing touches were being put on to Tanderagee Castle, it was reported by Samuel Lewis that Gosford's mansion was still far from com-pletion. By the 1850s the Norman-style castle, complete with battlements, towers and keep, was almost finished.[5] It has been suggested that the dark

1 Ariel view of The Argory

romanticism of its Norman style can be attributed to the influence of the earl of Gosford's wife, a close friend of Lady Byron who obviously shared the Byrons' romantic outlook.[6] As it was her money that funded most of the building work, it is quite possible that she had her say when it came to making decisions about style.

At the same time, just to the north of Armagh city across the River Blackwater in Co. Tyrone, the architect William Murray was remodelling Roxborough Castle, Moy, for the second earl of Charlemont. The original house was built in the late eighteenth century and in 1842 Murray was employed by Lord Charlemont to enlarge this existing house. He added a two-storey wing on either side, moved the entrance to the side of one of these wings and built a large group of outhouses.[7] Murray was also responsible for the building of nearby Castle Dillon, the 'large and austere' mansion of Sir George Molyneaux.[8] Lord Charlemont was clearly less than happy with Murray's work to Rox-borough; perhaps he felt that it failed to present the desired image, or lacked that touch of the exotic that was becoming so fashionable in the mid–nineteenth century. Whatever the reason, by the end of the 1850s the house had been transformed, this time by the Newry architect, William Barre. Barre, whose other work included the Ulster Hall and Albert Memorial in Belfast, further enlarged and embellished Roxborough, this time in a much more flamboyant manner.[9] Where mortgages could easily be taken out on estates, money was no obstacle for those who wanted to keep up with the fashions of the time.

It was not only the great landed families of Co. Armagh that were building at this stage. There were a number of smaller country houses being built too, the homes of baronets and 'landed gentlemen' rather than peers and nobles. One such was Churchill, described in 1838 by J.R. Ward of the Ordnance Survey as 'a handsome rectangular stone building, stuccoed, 4-storeys high'. He goes on to say of the house that 'the entrance through the demesne is pretty. The demesne and ornamental is extensive. The gardens are good and well laid out. There is a small collection of paintings, which are mostly portraits, and a good library.'[10] Churchill was built by the Verner family in the early 1830s to replace an earlier house which had existed on the same site. By this stage the Verner family were well established in the area, the first baronet, Sir William, having been at various times high sheriff of Monaghan, Armagh and Tyrone as well as representing Armagh county in Westminster for 36 years.[11] The new house at Churchill, tall, square and solid in design, was a fitting home for this respected member of society.

Another house is mentioned in the Ordnance Survey memoirs for the neighbouring parish of Clonfeacle:

> Derrycaw, the residence of W. McGeough Bond Esquire, situated on the banks of the Blackwater river, is a handsome modern house built with cut stone, with extensive office houses and a large garden. There are 92 acres of wood and young plantation.[12]

Positioned on a slight incline in a bend in the river, this was the house that became known as 'The Argory', its name thought to have derived from the Gaelic *ard garraidhe* meaning 'the hill of the garden'.[13] Like so many Ulster gentry houses it was modest in proportions, solid looking and yet with a quiet elegance. It gave the impression that it was going to be around for a while.

The Argory was built at the height of this period of mansion-building as a second home for the MacGeough Bond family, their principal family home being Drumsill, situated just outside Armagh on the main Dungannon road. The MacGeoughs had been in Co. Armagh for many years, holding much of their lands from the see of Armagh. As landowners, they were relatively modest. John Bateman's *Great landowners of Great Britain and Ireland*, first published in 1876, lists Joshua Walter MacGeough Bond of Drumsill House as owning a total of 5,624 acres, 3,992 of which were in Co. Armagh. This placed him as Armagh's fourteenth largest landowner, the largest being Lord Charlemont who owned 20,000 acres in Armagh and a further 5,000 in Tyrone. Joshua's younger brother, Captain Shelton, then resident at The Argory, had an estate of 2,451 acres attached to the property.[14] Unlike many of their neighbours, it would seem that their income did not come totally from rents, but was supplemented by wealth accumulated and carefully managed by earlier generations.

One of the earliest MacGeoughs to come to prominence was a Joshua MacGeough who is described in a late eighteenth-century document as 'an old Gentleman of the County of Armagh [who] had by laudable industry acquired a small Real Estate and a considerable personal fortune worth in the whole about £100,000'.[15] Joshua's son, William, had consolidated this wealth by marrying an heiress, Elizabeth Bond. They had one son, another Joshua, who inherited all their wealth and the family lands and rebuilt the family home at Drumsill between 1786 and 1788. This Joshua McGeough lived on at Drumsill until his death in 1817, and it was his curious will that was to lead to the building of The Argory.

For some reason Joshua disinherited his oldest son, William, leaving his estate instead to his second son, Walter, who was at that time practising as a barrister in Dublin. There was, however, a stipulation in the will. Walter was not allowed to bring a bride home to live in Drumsill House while two out of his three sisters remained unmarried and living there. As two of his sisters continued to show no signs of marrying and remained in excellent health, it became obvious that if he was ever to marry he would have to build another house for himself. The townland of Derrycaw in the Parish of Clonfeacle was chosen as the location for his new home – a perfect setting for a house, on good land and commanding views over the river and the surrounding countryside.

Walter employed as his architects John and Arthur Williamson of Dublin, probably on the recommendation of Francis Johnston, the famous Dublin architect who was a relative of Walter's mother and a native of Armagh. Work began in 1819 and by 1824 the house was completed – an elegant Georgian two-storey block with seven bays, built out of Caledon stone, faced with ashlar and trimmed with limestone from Navan. There were two storeys and seven bays with a breakfront centre bay. The main entrance faced west, overlooking the river, the front doorway being graced by a low arched fan light and a lion's head carved in the stone above the door. An extension was soon added to the north side of the house, consisting of a single storey passage leading to a two-storey octagonal pavilion. This was not to be the end of the alterations. In the early 1830s Walter MacGeough, who had by now added his paternal grandmother's name, Bond, to his own, extended the house again, raising the northern passage to two storeys and extending it beyond the pavilion by twelve two-storey bays. The main entrance was moved from the west front of the house, where it had a view of the river but was subject to wind and rain, to the more sheltered eastern side.[16]

The Argory, then, was one of many big houses that had been built, extended or elaborated by the landed class in this part of Ulster during the first half of the nineteenth century. The building that had been carried on in this area, in common with the rest of Ireland, was evidence of the confidence that these people had in their future place in Irish society and politics.

2 Captain Shelton
(courtesy of National
Trust)

Peers or minor gentry, landed magnates or owners of a few thousand acres, all shared a common belief that the years of peace and prosperity they enjoyed in the opening years of the nineteenth century would continue and that their place as leaders of the 'Irish nation' was assured. Thus they build their mansions, collected works of art from across the world, build up their libraries and planted and landscaped their demesnes.

What happened to these big houses and their families? What were the reasons for such a dramatic decline from the heady days of power and position in the 1870s to the desolation of the mid-twentieth century? Much has been written about the decline of Ireland's ascendancy and their houses, and many suggestions made as to the reasons for their demise. Historians such as T.W. Moody have placed great emphasis on the political develop-ments of the period[17] while others have stressed the importance of social or economic factors. J.E. Pomfret believed that the land struggle was a key factor, writing in 1930 that in most historical analyses the 'struggle for the land is lost sight of in the glamour of Home Rule. Yet it forms an equally vital portion of the history of the people during this period.'[18] In *Twilight of the Ascendancy* Mark Bence-Jones stressed the effect that the First World War had on the fate of many ascendancy families, with the loss of heirs to carry on the family name.[19] He also dealt with the devastating effects of the political revolution of 1916–21 and the Civil War, which saw the burning of many big houses. Terence Dooley has more recently highlighted the importance of the financial strain under which landlords increasingly found themselves at the end of the nineteenth and early twentieth centuries as income from rents almost disappeared but the cost of maintaining their houses and paying death duties and interest on loans remained unremitting.[20] Whatever the reasons, the fact remains that within little over half a century Ireland's landed class went from a position of undisputed social and political domination of society to one of being an irrelevant and sometimes persecuted minority.

A considerable amount of attention has been given to the fate of big houses in the south of Ireland, but what about their counterparts in the north? Was the picture the same in Ulster, or were different factors at work there? Certainly Pomfret argued that tenants in Ulster enjoyed much more favourable conditions in the decades after the Famine than did tenants elsewhere in the country and were thus less likely to be swayed by the message of the Land League. However, more recent research has suggested that Ulster tenants were just as discontented as their counterparts in the rest of Ireland.[21] A speech given by the lord chancellor in 1881 showed that the north of Ireland, far from being free from agrarian discontent, was at the heart of it and ripe for picking by the newly-formed League:

> It was in Ulster if anywhere that this land movement began. It is the greatest error in the world to say that this state of things was due to the land league. The land league was its effect, not its cause. The Land League would never have had the power which it acquired if it had no materials to work upon: the previous demand for legislative change which existed before the Land League, and nowhere more prominently than in Ulster.[22]

When the first challenges to the position of the Irish landed class arose in the early 1880s it would appear, therefore, that northern landlords were not to be spared but would be confronted with the same demands for rent reduction as those in the rest of the island.

Was this to lead to the economic ruin faced by many landed estates in the south? Would northern landlords experience the almost total political and social reversal witnessed by big house society elsewhere in Ireland? It would take a much more ambitious work than this to investigate the extent of the decline of big house society in the north. It is hoped, however, that by studying the experiences of one Ulster family, the MacGeough Bonds of The Argory, it may be possible to get an idea of the extent to which the developments of 1880 onwards affected the north as a whole. Exploring the variety of factors that determined the fate of this family and their home as well as that of neighbouring big houses in this part of mid-Ulster, may reveal the principal factors that operated to bring about the demise of big house society in the area.

While I make occasional reference to nearby mansions owned by Irish peers, the Argory, both in its character and in terms of the family that lived in it, was probably more typical of most big houses of the north of Ireland. Fairly unassuming in its proportions and home to a family that were 'minor gentry' rather than peers or nobles, The Argory in many respects epitomised the big house in the north of Ireland. A key element of this study, therefore, is to investigate why houses such as The Argory should have survived intact while many other of the grander big houses in the area have long since disappeared.

In carrying out my research for this work I have been helped greatly by the staff at the Public Record Office of Northern Ireland as well as at the Argory itself. There is a comprehensive and well-indexed collection of estate papers in PRONI, including family correspondence, solicitors' letters, rentals and official documents. These formed an essential part of my work, providing very necessary information concerning the practical and financial matters that affected various members of the family and the estate as a whole. The efficiency and courteousness with which these were always made accessible to me greatly facilitated my work. While this collection provided much of importance, the presence of a large number of papers of a more personal nature at the Argory itself added flesh to the dry bones of this work, enabling me to build up a clearer picture of the various family members. Diaries, letters and endless boxes of miscellaneous documents provided an insight into the character and the attitudes of individual family members. Now stored in a room set aside for archival material, the letter-books, diaries and notebooks are stored in chronological order, while the loose material and some miscellaneous books are kept in boxes labelled from A to E. This material is in the process of being copied, catalogued and stored away for preservation purposes. To the staff at the Argory who gave me free rein with this invaluable archive I am deeply indebted.

Sadly, a great number of earlier documents are thought to have been lost in a fire which destroyed the north wing of the Argory in 1898. The Octagon Room, now rebuilt but badly burned in the fire, had been used by both Walter – the builder of the Argory – and his heir, Captain Shelton, as a library in which they would have stored diaries, correspondence and official documents. If the papers left by later members of the family are anything to judge by, a great deal of value in terms of primary sources must have been lost on 3 June 1898. This has created a gap in the information available about life at the Argory between 1870 and 1898 but I have, as far as possible, tried to draw on other sources such as copies of their solicitors' correspondence, newspaper articles and some papers which would have been kept at Drumsill House.

Information regarding the other big houses in the Moy area was largely to be found in the private collections at PRONI, supplemented by the many interesting details provided by local people to whom memories of the big house have been passed down

1. The Argory in 1880

By 1880 The Argory had passed into the hands of Walter's second son, Ralph Shelton MacGeough Bond, the main family home of Drumsill having gone to his older brother, Joshua Walter. Ralph, who had for some reason reversed his name to Ralph MacGeough Bond Shelton, cut a dashing figure round this part of Co. Armagh. Born at Cheltenham in 1832, he had followed in the tradition of many Anglo-Irish families in attending Sandhurst and eventually serving in the army. For many younger sons of the big house, the continued expansion of the British empire would provide a splendid opportunity for travel and adventure. For others, service in the empire or the armed forces simply answered the problem of how to make a living.

Shelton had joined the 12th Lancers, and it was as a young cornet in this regiment that he had achieved fame for his bravery in one of the biggest maritime disasters of the nineteenth century. His was one of many regiments on board when, on 7 January 1852, Her Majesty's troopship *Birkenhead* sailed out of Cork harbour bound for South Africa and the Kaffir War, where reinforcements were desperately needed. As well as the 494 officers and men on board, many of whom were Irish, the ship carried 25 women and 31 children.[1] In the early hours of the morning, 26 February, the ship hit a reef two miles off the coast of South Africa. As the ship began to sink there was a frantic rush for the lifeboats and, in a true spirit of chivalry, the officers and men did all in their power to ensure the safe removal of women and children before they themselves took the few remaining spaces in the lifeboats. Shelton (then Cornet Bond) received special notice for having excelled himself in his display of courage. A painting of the sinking of the Birkenhead depicts him carrying two small children towards the lifeboats – according to several contemporary accounts, on going below to make a final check that there were no remaining women or children on the lower decks, Shelton found these two children and carried them to safety.[2] Shelton was one of the last to leave the ship, remaining on board until it went down. Most of the men perished in the freezing waters. Those who survived the cold were at the mercy of the sharks which swarmed to their easy prey, something which haunted Shelton as he remembered the events of that night:

> The sea at that time was covered with struggling forms, while the cries, piercing shrieks and shoutings for the boats were awful … Two men who were swimming close to me I saw disappear with a shriek, most probably bitten by sharks.[3]

Shelton managed to swim the two miles to shore, despite the freezing conditions and the sharks, finally struggling onto a beach through masses of thick seaweed. Apparently one of the first things he saw on coming round was his horse which had been thrown overboard and, miraculously, washed ashore. Many years later his nephew, Sir Walter MacGeough Bond, recollected:

> My uncle once told me that he partly attributed his having escaped the sharks to the fact that he did not, as many others did, take off his trousers to help him swim. The white flesh of the un-trousered attracted the sharks.[4]

Undeterred by his adventures, Shelton went on to fight in the Kaffir War to which the Birkenhead had been taking him. Several years later he fought in both the Crimean campaign and the Indian Mutiny and followed his adventures there by a spell in the Italian army. The final years of his military career saw him making quite a name for himself in the field of international diplomacy. Some of his duties included the carrying of despatches from the princess of wales to the king of Denmark who, most impressed with the young captain, had invited him to dine on several occasions.[5]

On inheriting The Argory, Captain Shelton, now retired from the army, had settled down to the tamer life of a landowner in Co. Armagh with surprising ease. Compared to the estates of some of his neighbours his lands were not extensive. As we have seen, the earl of Charlemont was by far the principal landowner, his Armagh estates extending to 20,695 acres with a value of £18,591. The other major landlords near to The Argory were Sir William Verner of Churchill who owned 5,436 acres and Sir James Stronge of Tynan Abbey with 4,402 acres.[6] Griffith's Valuation of 1867 shows that Walter had owned over 5,000 acres of land in Armagh. Many of these acres would have belonged to the family home at Drumsill and were passed on to Joshua, but there was still enough land attached to the Argory to ensure a comfortable income from rents. The Argory house and demesne sat on around 300 acres and with it Ralph inherited a variety of small estates in Armagh and elsewhere, accumulated through marriages or by acquisition earlier in the century. The 'Armagh Estate', which included the townlands of Tullymore, Edenderry, Culcairn, Artasooley, Pollinagh, Knockineagh, Ballymuckley, Mullintor and Kilcairn, extended to over 1,500 acres.[7] He also inherited the Altnamacken or 'Tipping' Estate in Armagh, the townlands of Ballynagross and Ballytrussan in Down and some land in Westmeath. Finally, Captain Shelton inherited a small estate in Wiltshire know as the 'Water Eaton Estate'.

Like an increasing number of landlords at this time, Shelton took a keen personal interest in the estate business. His diaries for 1892 show him at the age of sixty spending most days at the Argory overseeing the work, discussing details with his land steward, making his own cider and buying and selling

3 Captain Shelton in car with his chauffeur and butler 1913
(photo courtesy of National Trust)

cattle at the Moy fair. There was certainly a thriving, busy farm at The
Argory as the estate diaries show – there were harnesses to be taken to Moy
for repairing, tools to be sharpened and fuel to be transported. Day after day
men ploughed, collected stones, planted or lifted potatoes and spread
manure. The farm was important in that it had to support not just the
immediate family, but also the servants and any guests who might be staying.
The Argory was surprisingly self-supporting in terms of farm produce. Apart
from the obvious potatoes and carrots, there were strawberries, currents,
apples, and lime trees – they even tried germinating melon seeds in a hot
bed. This raising of exotic fruit and vegetable was not uncommon – the
greenhouses at Roxborough were famous for growing fruits such as pine-
apples and peaches[8] while, according to an historical article which appeared
in a local newspaper, Sir William Verner of Churchill 'employed seventeen
gardeners to help produce all manner of fruits and flowers'.[9] On 26 January

1891, a farm worker from The Argory took to Drumsill House a selection of produce including 'some turf, 4 rabbits, turnips, carrots, parsnips, artichokes, rhubarb, leeks, seakale, broccoli and celery'.[10] Butter, milk, pork and beef were also produced for consumption in the house.

With so much activity going on both on the estates and within the house, it is not surprising that The Argory and its neighbouring big houses had become significant local employers in the area around the village of Moy. Although at The Argory there was no need for the army of servants that would have been found at some of the grander houses, the smooth running of house and estate still depended on a large number of people. Not only were there many people employed on the estate but, as shown by an unreturned census form dated 7 April 1861, there had been nine servants living in the house on that day. These included a butler, footman, coachman and a stable helper. There was a Parisian dressmaker, and a cook who had been brought from Anne's native Westmeath. Finally there was a cook's assistant and two housemaids.[11] Interestingly, the census form showed that most of the servants came from the local area and all apart from one were Roman Catholics.

The servants lived comfortably, certainly when compared with the general living conditions of local labourers. Although most of the servants' quarters would have been in the North Wing, destroyed in the fire of 1898, the garret rooms above the main bedrooms are still there today, the names of many of the servants who lived there carved on the woodwork. These rooms were spacious, although cold and rather dark in winter owing to their attic location. The housekeeper and butler, thanks to their superior status, would have enjoyed more comfortable rooms located closer to the family quarters.

Captain Shelton seems to have been on very good terms with his servants, some of whom had been with the family for as long as he could remember. The Argory was a small enough house to be an intimate environment in which to live and the upper servants, in particular, had become an integral part of Shelton's life. The year 1898 started very badly for him when his butler, Ashton, took ill and was confined to bed. The anxiety he felt is apparent in the daily references he made to the state of Ashton's health – on 23 January he sent for Dr Deane who confirmed that Ashton had influenza. On the 28th Shelton had Dr Palmer, the family's doctor, called in for a second opinion. Nothing could be done, however. The entry for the 31 January 1898 reads: 'My old faithful servant who has been 35 years here died without pain at 9.30. His passing deeply regretted by all.' Later the same year another servant, Ballantine, took ill and died. Shelton, again, was most distressed by his death. Through much of the latter stages of his illness, Shelton had kept a nightly vigil over his bed. 'Poor faithful Ballantine died at 5 am,' he wrote on 28 August. 'He suffered greatly.'[12]

Eighteen ninety-eight was, truly, to be a dreadful year at The Argory. On 3 June Captain Shelton had been staying at Dover Place, Piccadilly when he received a wire from Allen informing him that there had been a fire at the Argory. The blaze must have been quite intense as the servants were still battling with it late the following day. Two days later saw Shelton back at the house, stunned by the damage. The entire north wing had been destroyed and at this stage it was impossible to tell what other structural damage had been done. What was perhaps worse than the damage to the building was the fact that the library and all its contents had been destroyed. These included all the diaries and letters of family members up to this point as well as a large collection of documents relating to the sinking of the *Birkenhead*. For the next few days, Shelton spent his time examining the damage, writing to the insurance company and discussing the events of that evening with each of the servants in an attempt to ascertain the cause of the disaster. He never did find out exactly who was responsible for the fire, but it was widely believed that the housekeeper had gone to bed leaving the fire in her room burning. A coal may have fallen out and smouldered on the floor, eventually licking into flames.[13]

For Captain Shelton the months after the fire were spent assessing the damage, deciding what was to be done in terms of repairs and beginning the long, difficult task of replacing some of the items that were lost. The first major decision that needed to be taken was whether or not to replace the twelve bay north wing exactly as it had been. In the end he decided not to have the full wing rebuilt, replacing it instead with a small wing of six bays. He commissioned the builder and contractor, Thomas McMillan of Ormeau Avenue, Belfast, to oversee the necessary repair work to be carried out over the next three years. Several receipts for the work still in existence at the Argory give an idea of some of the costs involved – McMillan's Summary of Accounts sent to Captain Shelton in 1902 came to a total of £3166 13s. 2d. A further £91 was paid to Riddel & Co., Ironmongers, for the repairs to the metalwork, while Musgrave & Co. of Belfast charged £50 for the installation of a new water heating apparatus with asbestos-lined pipes to heat the new wing.[14] On the eve of the New Year, Shelton, reflecting on the months just past, wrote in the back of his diary, 'The end of a most disastrous year. Ashton dead in Jan, house burned down on 3 June and Ballantine dead in August.' Apart from this dreadful year, however, life at The Argory continued on in its own quiet way, unaware of greater storms that lay just over the horizon.

For the majority of Irish landlords life in the 1880s was a healthy balance of work and recreation. Memoirs of big house life tell of house parties, dinners and lavish entertainment. Outdoor sports, in particular, provided an opportunity for physical activity as well as social interaction as gentlemen and ladies gathered in each other's houses for long weekends of sport and fun. Although the countryside in much of the north did not lend itself to that most famous of Irish pastimes, the hunt, this was more than made up for by the excellent shooting. Woodcock, grouse and pheasant were an important aspect of many a demesne, the duke of Abercorn once claiming that 12,644 woodcock had been shot at Baronscourt in a 40-year period.[15] While the Argory could not hope to equal this figure, the shooting parties provided ample entertainment for other gentry in the area. Hunting and shooting trips were often followed by dinner and an evening of quiet entertainment. On 8 November 1889 Shelton's guests included Major Alexander, Lord Louth, Captain Richardson and several other local personages. Their evening was spent playing whist and baccarat – welcome relaxation after a day's shooting in which they bagged 51 pheasants, 9 woodcock, 2 snipe and 11 rabbits.[16]

When not entertaining at The Argory, Shelton could often be found visiting some of the other big houses in the area. He maintained a close relationship with his brother and sister-in-law, spending many days with them over at Drumsill, or having them at The Argory for afternoon tea. He would occasionally have travelled to Tynan Abbey to visit the Stronges, while the Armstrongs of Dean's Hill, Armagh, were also close friends.[17] In the fairly exclusive nature of his friendships, Captain Shelton was typical of most Irish gentry who tended to choose their acquaintances from the small, elite social group to which they belonged. Interaction between the big house and the tenantry was limited to the occasional function given to mark a special event in the life of the family. Likewise, judging by the diaries of several of the MacGeough Bond family, interaction between members of the landed gentry and those titled peers who lived in the area was also fairly limited. Although Shelton would, in his old age, pay occasional visits to Lord Castle Stuart or Lord Charlemont, he would not have enjoyed with them that easy friendship that marked his relationship with the Stronges or Armstrongs. Social demarcations were still strong when it came to the people among whom the big house family chose their friends.

This exclusivity was not confined to social interaction; it also affected their choice of marriage partner. Rank was an important consideration when it came to this choice, as it was considered unacceptable to marry someone who was from a lower social class – unless, of course, they brought money into the family. As the number of gentry families living in Ireland decreased either in number or size, so finding a socially acceptable marriage partner became, in many cases, a great cause of anxiety. Although his relationship with his wife did not turn out to be a close one, Captain Shelton was considered fortunate in having found a wife in the daughter of Armagh landowner, Arthur N. Molesworth. The Argory, like so many Irish country houses, was far from the social activity of city life and, due to the physical difficulties involved in travel in those days, the reality was that unless they frequented the London or Dublin season, big house families tended to socialise mainly with neighbouring landlords and their families. For many, therefore, their choice of marriage partners was limited to the members of families within travelling distance.

As novelists and daughters of the big house, Edith Somerville and Martin Ross put it,

> to love your neighbour – or, at all events, to marry her – was almost inevitable when matches were a matter of mileage and marriages might have been said to have been made by the map.[18]

Most of the big house families close to the Argory had managed to make suitable connections. Sir William Verner of Churchill had married Harriet Wingfield of Powerscourt in 1819. Lord Charlemont was married to the Hon. Annette Handcock, daughter of the third Baron Castlemaine, while Lord Gosford chose for his wife the daughter of the duke of Manchester.[19] The MacGeough Bonds had not disgraced themselves, either. Shelton's brother, Joshua was now settled at Drumsill House with his wife, Louise Albertine Alphonsine Shanaghan. Louise was granddaughter of Michael Shanaghan, the architect of Downhill and travelling companion of Frederick Hervey, earl of Bristol. Shelton's youngest sister, Anne-Marie, married Randal Percy Otway Plunkett, Lord Louth of Louth Hall in Westmeath, and their son, the future Lord Louth, would spend many happy days at The Argory with his uncle Ralph. 'Marriage', writes Dooley, was 'an important means of regenerating the tightly-knit, exclusive nature of their community'.[20] Certainly the gentry in this part of the north were, for now, as keen as those elsewhere in Ireland to maintain that exclusive character, removed by marriage as by most other things from the Ireland that lived outside their demesne walls.

Shelton's own marriage to Caroline Molesworth had taken place on 1 May 1873, in St James' parish church, Moy.[21] Sadly, their union does not appear to have been a great success. She lived almost exclusively in Dublin, while he spent most of his time at The Argory, only visiting her for tea or taking her out for a ride in the park whenever he happened to be in the capital.[22] When Shelton was in Dublin he generally stayed at his club – a place where he could enjoy good food, a quiet atmosphere and the company of like-minded people. The club to which he belonged, the Kildare Street Club, was noted for its refined elegance as well as its unionist sympathies. In *Twilight of the Ascendancy*, Bence-Jones describes this club as 'the real centre of masculine Ascendancy life in Dublin'. He continues:

> Not only was [it] conveniently situated; it was luxurious and had the reputation of keeping the best table in Dublin. Oysters, when in season, were sent up daily from the Club's own oyster bed near Galway and cost members a shilling a dozen; muffins were sent from London. The cellar was of a corresponding degree of excellence, particularly with regard to champagne ... There were plenty of comfortable bedrooms for which the charge was three shillings and sixpence a night, so that the Club was a meeting place for gentlemen from all over the country.[23]

The club was where Captain Shelton would have met other landlords with whom, no doubt, the pressing issues of the day would have been discussed. Politics, in particular, would have been uppermost in the minds of many. As members of the main Dublin clubs were almost exclusively from the landed class, it was inevitable that some of them would have been leading figures in both local and parliamentary politics. Up until the 1870s the gentry totally dominated politics at all levels. Many landlords, their brothers, sons and nephews, represented their county in the Houses of Parliament; the first duke of Abercorn, for example, saw five of his sons take their seats as Members of Parliament in the House of Commons.[24] In 1868, 73 out of Ireland's 103 representatives at Westminster were members of the landed elite, while many of the rest were there as a result of a landlord's influence. Even those who did not aspire to these high echelons of power had their own duties as public representatives at a local level. Many of them were directly responsible for the administration of justice, presiding over the petty and quarter sessions in their capacity as justices of the peace. Others were deputy lieutenants or held positions on the boards of guardians. As well as having to fulfil these obligations, landlords also sat on a wide variety of committees and generally took a leading role in most local affairs. They had a tremendous amount of influence in the local community and some on a national level.

Captain Shelton and his neighbours were no exception, he himself having been a deputy lieutenant and JP for Co. Armagh. Sir James Stronge held the position of high sheriff for Co. Tyrone in 1880 and for Co. Armagh in 1885, while Lord Charlemont, as well as having been a JP and deputy lieutenant for Co. Tyrone, held the position of Comptroller of the Household to successive viceroys between 1868 and 1895.[25] For these men, as for others throughout the country, their role in public leadership was something they took completely for granted.

For many Irish landlords, this social and political responsibility was much less of a burden than that other great concern – money. There were those who managed their finances carefully, aware of the fine balance between income from rents and the expenditure necessarily associated with maintaining a country house and estate. There were others for whom money was something of which they needed huge amounts and never had enough. Although many landlords at that time were extremely wealthy, there were as many again for whom the appearance of wealth was an elaborate façade, hiding the reality of indebtedness and scarcity of ready cash. The cost of running an estate and maintaining a large country house, not to mention the expense involved in ensuring that they and their family were accoutred in a manner suited to their status in society, was often much greater than the amount being raised in rents.

Some spent prodigally either on themselves or their houses, bought the best horses, stayed in luxurious hotels across three continents and enjoyed the finest fare the world had to offer. The management of their finances was something they considered to be an inconvenient burden, one that some of them somehow managed to forget existed. Should rents fail to cover the cost of running their houses or paying for personal expenses, gambling debts or mounting mortgages inherited from ancestors, money was always available from other sources. Many landlords spent prodigally and borrowed heavily, confident that the economy would continue to grow. They borrowed not only from financial institutions but also from the church bodies, now flush from the fruits of disestablishment, and even from each other. At Churchill the Verners were using all means at their disposal to help them maintain their lifestyle, taking out mortgages from several landlords, including the MacGeough Bonds who had also loaned £15,000 to Lord Gormanston in the form of a mortgage on his estates.[26] While this was by no means the case for all landlords, there was a general carelessness regarding money as they continued to enjoy the fruit of the agricultural boom, giving little thought to the need for economic prudence. Times, it was felt, were good and getting better; there were more pressing things to think about than money. Dooley writes that most landlords

> had failed to exploit the commercial values of their estates by raising their rents in accordance with price increases, or continued to live extravagantly as if there was going to be no future downturn in the economy.[27]

Unlike a number of his neighbours, Captain Shelton was in quite a comfortable financial position. He did not have the enormous expenses associated with moving in high social circles; neither was he reckless in other ways with the family's resources. Apart from a few minor alterations, such as the installation in 1906 of an acetylene gas plant to provide lighting, he had made few changes to his house and certainly had no need for the large loans taken out by other landlords in the area. The large sums of money which had been brought into the family by advantageous marriages in the past were now safely invested in a variety of stocks, shares and loans to other landlords.

Some of his neighbours were in a less fortunate position. The earl of Charlemont, for example, was borrowing heavily. Much of his estate was heavily mortgaged as a result of debts accrued by his uncle and grandfather, both of whom had spent lavishly on building. The first earl, the 'Volunteer Earl' as he was known, had spent £60,000 on the building of his Casino at Marino, Dublin, in the 1760s. This, together with the renovations carried out on Roxborough House by the second earl, had been funded by the sale of large parts of the estate. By the time the third earl inherited there was not enough income from rents to cover the mounting debts and much of the remaining estate had to be mortgaged.[28] The earl of Gosford was likewise living well beyond his means. A.W.P. Malcolmson, in the introduction to his book on the Gosford papers in the Public Record Office of Northern Ireland, notes that as early as 1820 the estate had been in debt to the tune of £45,000. At this stage the third earl had ignored advice to cut back in his expenses, instead beginning work on the castle – work which was still in progress nearly 40 years later. He had also spent large amounts of money on building up an extensive library and died leaving the family finances in a sorry state. 'The Gosford family finances', writes Malcolmson, 'were probably ruined for ever by the building of Gosford Castle.' Shelton's contemporary, the fourth earl, was a close friend of the Prince of Wales, something that could also have devastating effects on a family's fortunes. It is said of the prince of Wales that

> Under his sway the upper classes would move between Newmarket, Ascot, the great country houses and London, indulging primarily in sport, good living and amorous intrigue.[29]

For Gosford to keep up with his set involved living well beyond his means, borrowing where he could in order to cover his huge expenses. He also gambled heavily, living, like many Irish landlords of the time, as if there would be no tomorrow.[30]

Despite these mounting debts, which for many were a matter of course, life for the gentry in this part of Ulster was continuing in 1880 much as it had always done. In common with landlords throughout Ireland, they continued to enjoy life on their estates or abroad, at the Club or entertaining and being entertained. Their position of social and political leadership went unchallenged and they were treated with deference and respect by tenants as well as members of the wider community. Few could guess at the changes which lay just over the horizon for landlords and tenants alike. Within a matter of years events were to unfold which would bring about not just the economic decline of the landed class, but the loss of the power and influence they had so long enjoyed.

2. Challenge to the landed interest, 1881–1914

When Gladstone visited Ireland in 1877 he had no idea that it was on the brink of yet another agricultural depression. The summer had been very wet and the harvest disappointing. One poor year would not have had a dramatic impact but, as is so often the way in Ireland, it was followed by several other equally bad years. As Ireland followed many parts of the world into economic depression, the value of agricultural goods dropped dramatically within a very short time. According to Vaughan the value of livestock and agricultural produce both fell by about 36 per cent while the value of crops was cut in half.[1] This had an almost immediate impact on the landlords as tenants quickly found themselves unable to pay their rents. On 22 October 1879 the MacGeough Bonds received the first of many petitions from the tenants in various townlands:

> We the undersigned tenants of your holdings in Tyrcarvedo humble [sic] beg leave to acquaint you that in consequence of our late and bad harvest and a complete failure in our potato crop and the low prices for our cattle, pork and all our farm produce that we find it impossible to pay the present rent due on the first of Nov. Now sir, hoping you will take these things into consideration and allow us a few months longer than the usual time to pay such amount as your noble heart may decide upon.[2]

Similar letters were to follow from Ballysheridan, Tullyvallen and Skerriff, and many other townlands. By March 1880 Lord Gosford's agent, William Wann, was feeling increasingly concerned by the situation: 'I am by no means plenty of money here & no prospect of the like … Rents coming in very slowly'.[3] Sir William Verner's agent, James Crossle, was also concerned. On 22 May 1880 he informed Sir William that

> we are doing all we possibly can and neither by threats or entreaties can we get money from the tenants who are still in arrear and an odd one is paying as soon as he can gather up his rent but a great many of the smaller tenants can barely manage to put a crop in the ground and won't be able to pay rent until harvest comes.[4]

For the tenant farmers, this downturn in their fortunes was devastating, bringing the prospect of ruin, eviction and even starvation. This was made more difficult by the fact that they had become accustomed to a relatively comfortable standard of living. As Donnelly has shown, 'With the exception of a few bad years in the early 1860s, Irish farmers enjoyed between 1854 and 1876 a degree of prosperity unparalleled since the French Revolution and the Napoleonic wars.'[5] Studies of agricultural output during the two decades since the Great Famine by historians such as Solow and Vaughan have shown that tenants had been doing very well indeed – much better, in fact, than the landlords. A survey of 50 Ulster estates carried out by Bardon has revealed that the average rent increase since 1853 had been only 20 per cent.[6]

This, combined with the high value of their produce, had increased tenants' expectations for the future, making the blow all the harder when it came. The economic crisis was to hit not only the tenant farmers: shopkeepers, bankers, merchants and the whole wider community felt the shock as the amount of available money fell. The combined effect of a world-wide depression and a second year's harvest failure caused deep anxiety in farmers for whom the horrors of the Great Famine were within living memory. This anxiety was soon to express itself in direct action against the landlords. Agricultural depressions had been a fairly regular occurrence in Ireland's history, as had times of agrarian unrest, but this time was to be different. As Comerford has shown, the result of this depression 'was not only agrarian unrest, but a political movement that was to overturn Gladstone's and everyone else's assumptions about Irish politics'.[7] What was it that turned this potential unrest into revolution? The answer lies in the fact that for the first time in Irish history an economic crisis coincided with the emergence of strong political leadership of the people.

On 21 January 1881 in Kinnegoe, Co. Armagh, not that far from The Argory, a gathering of two thousand farmers were addressed by Michael Davitt who told them,

> You are no longer the tame and superstitious fools who fought for their amusement and profit with your equally foolish and superstitious Catholic fellow workers … No, my friends, the landlords of Ireland are all of one religion – their God is Mammon, and rackrents and evictions are their morality.[8]

The Land League had reached Co. Armagh and brought with it the demand not only for a reduction in rents, but for the very destruction of landlordism. Davitt, a former revolutionary and land activist, had in 1879 joined forces with Charles Stewart Parnell in what became known as the New Departure. Together they formed the organisation that would do much to bring landlordism to its knees. The driving, charismatic leadership of Davitt with his revolutionary background and Parnell who, being from a highly regarded landlord family, commanded respect from all classes, was sufficient to motivate tenant farmers across Ireland regardless of their religious persuasion

In June 1879 the earl of Charlemont had written from his London address to Hugh Boyle, agent for the Co. Armagh estate:

> I send two cutting from a paper, *The Standard*, sent here. I fear both indicate bad times for landlords ... As for this meeting in Mayo and the demand first for reduction and then, no doubt, for refusal of rent, there was no doubt the Home Rule party would come to such a programme before the next election. The rents in the South and West are far in excess of the valuation, and it may be some time before the North can be made to reduce.[9]

His words were soon to seem over-optimistic. It quickly became apparent that the tenants in many parts of Armagh and Tyrone were as ready as any others to heed the message of the Land League during the difficult months of 1880–1. During the severe weather of 1879, many farms in Co. Armagh had been totally flooded, depriving the farmers of both food and shelter. This part of Armagh close to Lough Neagh has always been particularly susceptible to flooding. The tenants here had been hit very badly by the atrocious weather conditions and could not find the money to pay their rents. Their response was to either demand a reduction or refuse to pay their rents at all. Sir William Verner's agent complained that:

> we are getting on very badly with rent receiving ... The people are so excited by the infernal Tenant League agitators that they hardly know what to do and I regret to say it is not exclusively confined to the Roman Catholics. Many Protestants are just as bad.[10]

The Verners were faced with the same problem as most landlords in other parts of the country – how to deal with tenants who could not or would not pay. Did you evict them and replace them with tenants who might pay the rents or keep them on and have no income from that holding? Wholesale evictions, Crossle believed, would have a detrimental effect. Writing to the London solicitors, Jackson and Prince, he outlined the difficulties:

> Believe me we are doing all in our power to get in the arrear of rent. Of course we shall have to evict some of the tenants heavily in arrear and to levy the amount of decrees upon others but this must be done with care and judgement. If attempted in a wholesale way, we should have a combination against us not merely of Sir William's own tenantry but of the whole people of the country.[11]

The alternative was to offer the tenants a reduction in rent and this seems to have been the course most commonly adopted by landlords in general.

Although there were those like the infamous John George Adair of Donegal
who refused to grant any reductions, most landlords accepted that their
tenants were not in any position to pay and that lower rent was better that
no rent. Lord Gosford, for example, granted a reduction of 10 per cent in
Armagh and 15 per cent in Cavan.[12]

Tenants' demands were, however, becoming increasingly insistent. 'The
duke of Manchester's tenants and Lord Lurgan's have modestly asked a
reduction of 50 per cent! And I see Mr Hancock (Lord Lurgan's agent) has
been threatened,' Crossle wrote to Jackson.[13] By January 1881 Sir William
Verner's tenants were becoming organised:

> Four men, two Protestants and two Catholics have been going round
> the tenantry warning them not to pay until they get a further donation
> from Sir William,' Crossle informed Jackson, 'I believe a second peti-
> tion has been sent from here demanding a further reduction. I heard
> that less than 25 [per cent] will not content them.[14]

Lord Gosford's agent was dealing with a similar situation:

> I have just heard from His Lordship in reply to the memorial from the
> tenants asking for a larger abatement and he has allowed me to give 5 per
> cent more than he had at first authorized which will make the abate-
> ment on the year's rent to Nov.'80 to be 20 per cent or 4s. in the £.[15]

The situation was the same throughout the country as, for the first time,
landlords were facing the reality that tenants could and would refuse to pay
the rents demanded of them.

Under mounting pressure from Ireland, Gladstone reacted to the worsening
situation by the introduction of a bill that was to be of great significance for
Ireland's tenants, transforming the relationship between them and their landlords. In the passing of Gladstone's second land act of 1881, the government
finally acknowledged the Irish tenants' need for greater security of land
tenure, granting the 'three f's' which they had for so long been demanding –
fixity of tenure, fair rents and freedom of sale. The act had long-term
implications for tenants and for landlords as it would introduce a dual system
of land ownership in which the landlords still owned the land but their
powers were greatly reduced. The most important outcome for the moment,
however, was the fact that the act ordered the establishment of special land
courts that were to be set up throughout the country for the purpose of
settling new fair rents. This was what tenants wanted to hear and, for the
months following the establishment of the Land Commission courts, tenants
flocked to them in the hope of having their rents permanently reduced.
Between August 1881 and December 1902 the sub-commissioners dealt

with 342,019 cases in which rents were fixed. In nearly every case the rent was fixed at a level well below what they had been – on average at around 15 or 20 per cent below their previous level, but occasionally as much as 33 per cent lower.[16]

Needless to say, the outcomes of these hearings were uppermost in the minds of the agents and landlords alike. This was a time of great anxiety for many landowners; here was entirely new legislation and, as is usually the case, there was intense speculation as to how they would be affected. The worst case scenario, as landlords saw it, was that all the tenants on an estate would seek and be granted substantial reductions in their rents. This would, in effect, bring about a drop in their income of somewhere between 15 to 30 per cent. For those whose finances were already strained, this was indeed an alarming prospect. On 22 October Crossle informed Sir William Verner that

> All the tenants in Ireland are anxiously watching the proceedings in the new Court, and if there is anything to be gained they will *all* take advantage of it. It is the most important and critical time that has ever occurred in Ireland. All depends on the Commissioners and I confess I distrust them. Gladstone's object is to rob the landlords.[17]

Sir William was one who quickly felt the impact of this drop in rental income. He was not only in debt to various people, including, as we have seen, the MacGeough Bonds; he also had a number of family dependants whose allowances needed to be paid out of this income. His mother, Lady Verner, was particularly impatient with any interruption to her steady supply of money. Crossle, as agent to the family, had the unenviable task of dealing on one hand with discontented tenants who were demanding a reduction in their rents, while on the other hand attempting to manage the expectations of irate family members who were insisting on having money that just was not there; all the while trying to ensure the continued smooth running of the estate. Correspondence between Crossle and the Verners, who were still living in London, was becoming increasingly fraught as bills mounted and rents still did not come in. In reply to an angry letter from Lady Verner, Crossle wrote in May 1882

> I respectfully submit there is not one word of suggestion in my letter as to economy on your part. I am well aware that you have been endeavouring to keep down expenses but I thought it my duty to draw attention to the fact that expenses and outgoings are *in advance of the receipts* which is the cause of the great difficulty in meeting the interest and compulsory charges upon the property. Of course we will do all in our power to pay the interests but if it has to be taken to meet other demands, how are we to do so?[18]

The Verners had always enjoyed an expensive lifestyle and, in common with many landowners throughout Ireland, were finding it hard to adjust to their new financial situation. In the past it had always been possible to borrow more money in order to maintain their standard of living. Mortgages were taken out on properties without a second thought if necessity demanded it. Now they were finding themselves in a position where the interest payments still had to be made but the money was not there to pay them.

Furthermore, it was becoming almost impossible to find anyone prepared to lend to an Irish landlord at this time. Samuel Hussey wrote an article to *The Times* in which he claimed that 'No capitalist will now lend on Irish estates as they naturally argue if the government forcibly reduces rents in an exceptionally good year, what in a bad year?'[19] The Verners, for example, were refused a loan by their bank. 'The manager,' Crossle explained to Sir William, 'is most anxious to oblige but said "he feared the Directors (who are all English or Scotch) would not advance money to an *Irish landlord*"!'[20] After several failed attempts they found a private individual willing to lend them £60,000 on their estates in Tyrone, Armagh and Monaghan at a rate of 4¼ per cent interest payable half-yearly. This would enable them to pay off all their other creditors, including the MacGeough Bonds, who were pressing heavily for payment of interest on their loans.[21]

The experiences of the nobility and gentry around the Armagh area at this point seem to have been fairly representative of the situation generally in the north. While some of the large older estates were severely hit by the impact of Gladstone's land act of 1881, the smaller estates of the minor gentry seem to have weathered that particular storm slightly better. There is certainly no indication at this stage that the MacGeough Bonds were experiencing anything like the same financial difficulties as some of their grander neighbours. There seem to have been a number of reasons for their relative security, the most important of which was the fact that they were not totally dependant on rental income but had quite a large amount of capital invested in a variety of ways. In this they were similar to a large number of smaller landlords in the north.

Some, particularly those who lived in Cos. Down and Antrim close to the industrial centre of Belfast, were recent recruits to the ranks of landed gentry, having made enough money out of the booming industries of the city to enable them to buy up a small country estate and build or restore a suitable mansion on it. The same was to be found close to the north's provincial towns such as Lisburn or Dungannon. The Youngs of Galgorm Castle, for example, had been successful Ballymena merchants who had taken advantage of the breakup of the earl of Mountcashel's Antrim estates in 1850 to acquire a country estate and the social prestige attached to it.[22] Further north, the estate at Drumnasole had been bought by the Turnly family in 1808. Francis Turnly, having made his money in the far east, returned to buy the estate for £7,400 payable in gold![23] Many of these families either had substantial sums invested or had retained a certain interest in business ventures. Furthermore, they were less likely have the heavy financial drain of mortgages or large annuities to family members that left many of the older estates struggling. For these minor gentry families, therefore, the loss of tenanted land did not have nearly the same impact as it had on some of the older estates of Ireland's peers.

Many of Ulster's minor gentry also tended to be more financially astute than some of the older landed families. As we saw in the introduction to this book, the MacGeough Bonds, for example, had always shown a degree of canniness when it came to money. Their industry, as well as their fortunate choice of marriage partners, meant that by the beginning of the nineteenth century they had built up a sizeable fortune. Unlike, for example, the Gosfords, Walter had been easily able to afford to build The Argory without compromising the family's financial security. Unfortunately it is impossible to discover how much he left to his sons on his death as no copy of his will has survived. His wife's will was preserved, however, and from it can be ascertained the fact that she had brought to the family 'certain sums of money' specified in her marriage contract of 16 June 1830. She left 'the said sums of money or the investments for the time being representing the same' to her son, Ralph MacGeough Bond Shelton. The value of her estate on her death was declared to be £53,840 3s. 1d. before any deductions.[24] The combined legacies of his mother and father would have provided Shelton with a healthy amount of capital which he invested in a wide variety of stocks and shares. On his death in 1916, the annual income of Captain Shelton's residuary estate was estimated to have been £5,278 9s. 8d. Of this only around £1,900 was from rents while the income from his investments totalled £3,387.[25]

It would seem, too, that the rents on Captain Shelton's estate did continue to come in on a fairly regular basis. In 1889 the estate rentals show that the Westmeath estate brought in a total of £680, with nothing owed in arrears, while the County Down estate had arrears of £30 10s. out of a total of £696. The rent book for 1899, ten years later, shows that on his Armagh estate only five out of his 84 tenants were in arrears.[26] Of even greater importance to the MacGeough Bonds, however, was the fact that they also had an estate in England. Situated near Crickdale in Wiltshire, the Water Eaton estate consisted of two large, prosperous farms from which rents continued to come in on a regular basis. The security of a steady income which these English estates provided at this time was invaluable. There was little fear that the tenants there would be affected by the land agitation spreading through Ireland. The Water Eaton estate also provides an interesting variant on the perception of the absentee Irish landlord living on some estate in England. Captain Shelton, like many others, was absent from his English estate much preferring his Irish home!

Not only were the MacGeough Bonds protected from the worst of the reduction in rental income, but compared to the Verners, the Charlemonts or the Gosfords, Captain Shelton seems to have lived very much within his means. There were, of course, the usual expenses associated with the maintenance of a large country house. Heating costs, alone, would have been considerable. The servants also had to be paid; at The Argory there would have been between eight and ten household servants creating an annual wage bill of over £250. At this stage the family also employed over 20 estate workers.[27] For Captain Shelton there was also the additional expense incurred by the fire in 1898. However, unlike many landlords for whom a fire provided a wonderful opportunity to have their house embellished in grand style, Shelton seems to have just carried out basic repair work, as has already been noted. The original twelve-bay north wing was replaced by a shorter one of six bays and the style was kept simple. At this stage Captain Shelton would have been 67 years old. He and his wife had had no children to inherit the property and it is probable that he would have had little heart in spending large amounts of money on grand building schemes, especially at a time when the future of Irish landowners was looking so uncertain.

Table 1. Payments made by Captain Shelton, November 1899

Tithe rent charge, parish of Killyman	£3	8	1
Tithe rent charge, parish of Clonfeacle	£71	8	10
Tithe rent charge, Armagh see	£145	14	8
Tithe rent charge, parish of Armagh	£41	7	4
Lough Neagh Drainage	£4	1	0
Irish Game Protection Association	£1	1	0
Protestant Orphan Association	£5	0	0
Moy Church Sustentation Fund	£10	0	0
The Armagh Club	£3	0	0

Source: PRONI, D/288/G/2

Neither did Captain Shelton have the hefty expenses which came with the struggle for public position – unlike his neighbour, Sir William, who had great difficulty paying off the costs accumulated by his election campaign. For many landlords, the ambition to sit in Parliament created a constant drain on their financial resources. The MacGeough Bonds, on the other hand, preferred a quieter existence, doing their public duty on a local level but not getting involved in the struggle for public position that left so many of their contemporaries in financial difficulty. For other landlords in Cos. Armagh and Tyrone, however, the land agitation and the reduction in rental income as a result of the land act brought a tremendous financial strain from which some families would not recover.

The social revolution that was changing the face of land ownership in Ireland was beginning to make itself felt in other ways, too. As we have seen, up until this time landlords had occupied all the important positions in local as well as national politics. They were magistrates, deputy lieutenants, poor law guardians and members of grand juries. Their right to represent the people in Westminster went undisputed – of the two MPs returned from each county as well as the eleven from the boroughs, the vast majority were from a landed background. Sir William Verner represented Armagh county at Westminster from 1873 to 1880[28] while the town of Dungannon was represented by Col. Knox and the city of Armagh by Capt. C. de la P. Beresford, all of whom were staunchly conservative.[29] For decades the pattern had been the same. Now it was all set to change, not only in Ireland but in Great Britain where the established view that the landed interest had an automatic right to represent the people would become increasingly challenged. In Ireland, however, the land issue acted as a catalyst which would bring about that change with a rapidity and totality that was breathtaking.

In the general election of 1880 opposition to the landed, conservative interest was organised in every county and nearly every borough in Ulster and for the first time the challenge would be successful.[30] The general discontent felt among tenants was beginning to extend to their willingness to be led in political issues. This growing independence from their landlords was aided by the fact that the ballot act of 1871 now gave tenants the right to cast their vote in secret. Although it was still considered by many to be their duty to vote according to the declared wishes of their landlord, an increasing number of tenants, encouraged by the land league, voted for the candidate they felt best represented their interests. The results of the election demonstrate the impact that the issue of land reform was having in the country. Across the three southern provinces of Ireland the landlords were routed.[31] In Ulster, too, although not so total, the political influence long enjoyed by the landed class was being seriously eroded.

However, although many Catholic and Protestant voters had united over the land issue and elected liberal candidates in many constituencies, the national issue was about to divide politics in Ulster along very different lines. As far as many Ulster tenants were concerned, the land act of 1881 had given them much of the security they desired. The increasingly nationalist agenda of the Land League was beginning to alienate a significant proportion of those protestant tenants who had previously given them support and who, although desirous of land reform, were essentially unionist in their politics. Captain Shelton's nephew, Walter, recorded in his diary for September 1883 an event which demonstrates the growing antagonism being felt by the Orange Order in Armagh and Tyrone towards the message of the Land League:

Went to Dungannon. The Orangemen held a meeting in the market place to protect against the Parnellite party and to show their loyalty to the British connection. T.P. O'Connor, T. Healy and O'Brien came down to address a meeting and tried to force their way to the market place where the Orange meeting was being held, but were prevented doing so by the police and soldiers (foot and horse). The National Speakers had to be escorted through the streets back to the Ry. Station; for the Orangemen would have mobbed them.[32]

In the general election which took place two years later this division on the Home Rule issue became even more apparent. In North Armagh the Orangemen, many of whom had earlier lent their support to the Land League and voted for liberal candidates who advocated reform, now voted determinedly for the conservative candidate of their own chosing, Major Edward Saunderson. Nationalists, meanwhile, saw in the new Home Rule movement the only effective representation of their political aspirations and, north and south, voted overwhelmingly for Home Rule candidates.

The 1885 general election saw landlords throughout the southern provinces of Ireland losing even more of their hold on the reins of power – out of the 103 seats, Parnell's Home Rule party took 85.[33] The landlords of Ulster, however, managed to retain some vestige of influence. The general elections of 1885 and 1886 saw a swing back to the Conservative Party as the only security against the growing threat of Home Rule. 'The Conservatives,' writes Walker, 'emerged from the elections as the exclusive representation of non-nationalist opinion in Ulster, and, surprisingly in the light of social developments over the last decade, the Tory MPs were drawn almost entirely from the gentry.'[34]

Many Ulster landlords became involved in the unionist fight against home rule, Captain Shelton being no exception. On the night of 19–20 April 1914 supporters of the recently formed Ulster Volunteer Force secretly landed 216 tons of arms at Larne, Bangor and Donaghadee from where they were taken on by cars to prepared dumps all across Ulster. The convoy of cars travelling to the south and west of the province turned off the main road just before Dungannon and began winding its way along the narrow country roads leading to The Argory. Turning in at the main gate, the cars crept up the driveway and stopped outside the house. Now, well away from any main roads and totally hidden from view, it was safe for the drivers to stop. Much-needed rest and refreshments were then provided for everyone before the convoy continued its journey in the small hours of the morning.[35]

Captain Shelton was not alone in allowing his property to be used by the Ulster Volunteers. Other landlords had used their demesnes for drilling – a photograph of rows of uniformed volunteers standing to attention in the main courtyard is still on display in Killyleagh Castle. Donard Park, also in Co.

Down, was used for the same purpose. Close friends of the MacGeough Bonds, the Lennox-Cunninghams, allowed their demesne at Springhill to be used, while further north at Newtownstewart the Tyrone regiment 'camped at Baronscourt for a weekend in October 1913, consuming a ton of potatoes and 1,470 pounds of beef, and were given squad, battalion and musketry drill, and a lantern-slide lecture on the South African War'.[36]

Politically the landed gentry of Ulster still had their part to play, especially in this new struggle against Home Rule, but it was a part that was no longer considered theirs by right. From now on they were answerable to a progressively independent and politically aware electorate. They would still be returned by constituencies but only provided they were prepared to represent the views of the people. The days when, in the words of Walker, 'the proprietors expected to give a lead and the tenants accepted their right to do so' were gone for good.[37]

3. Decline and fall, 1914–45

By 1916 Captain Shelton, now 85 years of age, was becoming too feeble to travel far. On Sunday 6 February he recorded in his diary that the Revd Archer had come to The Argory to administer Holy Communion. The day, he noted, was stormy. On the following day Mr Orr and Dr Palmer lunched with him. For each of the next four days the entry in the diary simply reads: 'In bedroom'. After 11 February the diary is blank. One month later, on 10 March, the *Irish Times* recorded in its obituaries the death of 'the gallant Captain Ralph MacGeough Bond Shelton D.L., which occurred on Wednesday evening at his residence, The Argory, County Armagh.' Captain Shelton had died suddenly and peacefully in the house he loved, with just a few servants there to attend to him. A local paper reported on his funeral:

> On Monday the remains of Ralph MacGeough Bond Shelton of The Argory, Moy, the last survivor of the wreck of the Birkenhead, were laid to rest in the family vault in Armagh Cathedral. Deceased was a popular and liberal landlord, and a friend to the residents of the district, so that many joined the cortege. Owing to the war it was impossible to provide the usual gun carriage and cavalry escort.[1]

In many ways the death of Captain Shelton marked the end of an era for The Argory. Life there no doubt had been affected by the political and economic changes that had rocked the Irish countryside, but the long-term repercussions had yet to be felt. Neighbouring landlords may have been struggling with their finances, faced with the necessity of selling off their estates, but for Captain Shelton and the servants and estate workers at The Argory life went on much as it had always done. On the estate, despite his infirmity, Shelton had taken an active interest in all that was going on, spending most days being wheeled around the estate in his bath chair. In 1911, at the ripe old age of eighty and with almost total loss of the power in his legs, his social life had still been remarkably busy. On 28 August of that year he had held an organ recital in the upstairs gallery of the house. For 18 September his diary reads, 'Motored to Glasslough Fete. Took my wheelchair on the top …' Several days later he 'Motored to Gosford Castle and lunched with the Gosfords & saw baby heir' while on October 9 he visited both Viscounts Charlemont and Castle Stewart.

Servants and workers were, as we have seen, valued and respected. The house, now restored after the fire, was lived in and cared for. On his death it

4 Sir Walter MacGeough
Bond in 1891 (photo
courtesy of National Trust)

was reported of Captain Shelton that 'everyone in and about The Argory
loved him. He was their best friend and happiest when in the midst of his
people and seeing them enjoying themselves, and to their enjoyment he was
always contributing'.[2] He loved The Argory and, although he had no sons of
his own to inherit the property it was his wish that it should always remain in
the family. Less than a month before his death, however, he discovered that his
younger nephew, Ralph Francis Xavier MacGeough Bond, to whom he had
planned to leave the property, refused to consider living at The Argory. Rather
than have the house and demesne either fall into decay or be sold off to
strangers, Shelton altered his will in favour of his elder nephew, Walter, provided
he agreed to reside for part of each year at The Argory.[3]

Walter Adrian MacGeough Bond, who had already inherited Drumsill
House in 1905, was following a successful career as a judge in Cairo when
the news reached him of his uncle's death. Educated at Christchurch, Oxford
and then in Germany, he was called to the Inner Temple in 1884 after which
he took up a post as advocate in Cairo. There he became first a judge and
then vice-president of the Court of Appeal. He was well-respected and was
honoured for his work there with a second class 'Madjdie', second class
'Osmanieh' and second 'Star of the Nile'.[4] On 21 February 1917, a year after
he inherited The Argory, Walter's services in Cairo were recognised by a
knighthood, conferred on him by the king at Buckingham Palace.[5] It was

while working in Cairo that Sir Walter had become friendly with the lady who was to become his wife – Ada Nichols, daughter of Charles Nichols of Dunedin, New Zealand. Nichols was a wealthy man, having been a founding member of the successful firm, Dalgety, Nichols & Co., and his assets enabled Ada to maintain her financial independence throughout her married life. She and Walter were married in St Saviour's Church, London, on 26 September 1901. Sadly, however, their marriage would not be a happy one. Although they did have a son, Neville, their relationship was to be one of mutual resentment and eventual animosity.

By 1916, while Sir Walter continued to pursue his career in Egypt, Ada and their son Neville, or 'Tommy' as he was known, had been living either on the continent or near her family in Doneraile, Co. Cork, occasionally travelling north for a short stay at Drumsill House. They did, however, continue to correspond on a regular basis – indeed, Sir Walter had received a letter from her a few weeks before Captain Shelton died keeping him informed of his uncle's state of health. Ada and Tommy had travelled up to Drumsill from Cork and had gone at once to The Argory:

> Uncle Ralph looked & spoke better than I had expected to find. But he must be dreadfully weak & tired out. He says he hasn't the least wish to get better & that he isn't a bit nervous about it. In fact he is making all the arrangements himself, so Dr Palmer tells me … There are great floods on the way to the Argory. I thought one was a lake that had escaped my notice before.[6]

Just weeks later, the judge received news of his uncle's death. It took some time to wind up his affairs in Egypt, to formally resign from his position and to say farewell to his associates and acquaintances. Finally, on 21 June, he left Cairo and began his long journey to the very different world of Co. Armagh and his new life as an Irish landlord. By 17 July Sir Walter had arrived in Dublin where he met with Mr Orr, the long-suffering partner of Beauchamp and Orr, solicitors, who was to become advisor on all matters relating to his property, his finances, and life in general. On 21 July 1916, Walter MacGeough Bond drove up the tree-lined avenue of The Argory for the first time as its owner.

The Ireland to which Sir Walter had returned was, like The Argory, in the midst of great change. For the gentry, the golden glow of the Edwardian era had already been brought to an abrupt end on the battlefields of France and Belgium; there were few big houses unaffected by the seemingly unending loss of life. The heir to Glasslough, Norman Leslie, and Sir George Brooke's son and heir were both killed in action in October 1914. The following month saw the deaths of the duke of Abercorn's brother and, on the same day, Lord O'Neill's son and heir.[7] The MacGeough Bonds were not untouched,

5 Lady Ada previous to her marriage (photo courtesy National Trust)

either. On 29 August 1917, Sir Walter recorded in his diary that he had just received news of the death of his nephew, Ralph, only son of his brother who was to have inherited The Argory on Captain Shelton's death. Stuck into the space for that day is a newspaper cutting – one which was only too familiar for so many families:

> Second Lieutenant Ralph Shelton MacGeough-Bond R.F.A., who died of wounds on August 22, was the only son of Lieutenant-Colonel and Mrs. MacGeough Bond, Leasbrook, Monmouth, and was 19 years of age.[8]

Momentous events were also unfolding close to home, events which were to have a lasting impact on Irish politics. In May 1916, while Sir Walter was preparing to leave Cairo for Ireland, he received a letter from his wife, then living in Dublin.

> It has been an anxious time but of course we were only on the outskirts – but we saw a terrible glow in the sky for a couple of days & that was enough combined with the constant firing to let us know what was going on. All communication of all sort was cut off. I tried to get news of Aunt Mary when I heard of the fighting in Stephen's Green but I failed & I do not know where she is or how … I hope to go north as soon as possible although I have not been able to get any servants owing no doubt to the Revolt … It's a bad business. I hope they'll shoot people like Casement.[9]

Already the catalyst for deep political division, the political repercussions of the Easter Rising and the subsequent execution of its leaders would become fully apparent two years later in the general election of 1918. In this election Sinn Fein would take 73 seats compared to the mere 6 seats won by the parliamentary party and the Unionists would increase their numbers to 26.[10] Already, however, there was only one issue in Irish politics – the establishment of an Irish Republic and whether or not Ulster would be excluded from it.

Even before war and political revolution conspired to turn the world of the big house on its head, the position of the Irish landlord had been transformed by the combination of successive land acts and loss of political power. The land act of 1881 had, as we have seen, facilitated the tenant in having his rents fixed for a 15 year period by the new land courts. This had been followed by the Ashbourne Act of 1885 which allowed landlords to sell their tenanted land at a price fixed by the government. Although the terms were attractive to neither tenant nor landlord,[11] there were some landlords who gladly took the opportunity to sell some of their outlying estates in an attempt to pay off some of their more pressing debts. A further land act two years later encouraged a greater sale of land.

It was the Wyndham Act of 1903, however, which had brought about the greatest change in land ownership – what Moody has described as 'the greatest revolution in the history of modern Ireland'.[12] Like the Ashbourne Act, it enabled landlords to sell to their tenants but with the great incentive of a 12 per cent bonus to the landlords. For the tenants the deal they were being offered was irresistible, and it was in the years following this act that most tenants bought their land. For landlords, many of whom were mortgaged to the hilt and struggling to make ends meet, there was really no choice. There were few who were in a position to resist the offer of the bonus and Bence-Jones writes that 'by 1914 three-quarters of the former tenants had bought their holdings'.[13] The MacGeough Bonds, as we shall see, had already sold off some of their lands and, in the decade that was to follow, Sir Walter would part with much of what was left.

Events abroad and at home were, for Sir Walter, of less immediate concern than the running of his new property. There was much that needed sorted out, both in terms of the estate and, more importantly from Walter's point of view, his finances.

Despite the comparatively comfortable financial position of the family, Sir Walter was ever anxious about money and kept a close eye on every penny – much to the oft-expressed disgust of his wife. It was to be a subject that would occupy his thoughts to a large extent over the next few years, especially as other landed families in the area were so obviously struggling for survival.

At Churchill, for example, the once respected Verner family had by now all but died out in a state of dissolution and poverty. On the untimely death of Sir William Verner in 1886 the estate had passed to his wife's illegitimate son, Harry, to whom Sir William had insisted on giving the Verner name. The estate was already heavily encumbered by annuities and mortgages, and had been badly hit by the rent strikes of the early 1880s.[14] One of the first things Harry Verner did on succeeding to the estate was to sell off most of his Tyrone estates under the terms of the 1891 land act. The rest were to be sold off within a matter of years under the better terms of the Wyndham Act.[15] For many landlords, the 12 per cent bonus allowed them on the sale of their estates under the Wyndham Act was carefully invested. For others, however, the availability of ready cash was an opportunity to live it up as never before and many such bonuses were lost on the gaming tables of Europe.[16]

On coming to Churchill, Harry reputedly declared it his aim to enjoy a life that was short but merry. Apparently he did just that, with Churchill becoming the venue for many a wild party, where drinking, gambling and cockfighting were the order of the day. It is obvious that he enjoyed the good life and, with the sale of his estates, there was nothing to stop him, for now. When not at Churchill, Harry, like Sir William before him, enjoyed the social life of London, where he spent most of his time. His badly depleted funds could not sustain this lifestyle for long and in 1898 Churchill was put up for sale, the London residence already having been sold in order to pay off a £60,000 debt inherited from his stepfather.[17] The house did not sell but a contents auction in 1902 managed to raise some more funds by selling off all the furnishings and paintings collected by generations of Verners. It was at this auction that Captain Shelton bought the two bronze statues of dogs by Fratin which still grace the west hall at The Argory.[18] All was to no avail, however, and by December 1913 Harry Verner was facing bankruptcy.[19]

For the Gosfords of Markethill things were also looking very bad indeed. During the 1880s, as we have seen, Lord Gosford had been forced to give a substantial reduction in his rents. This was the last straw for an estate already deeply in debt. The castle which had cost so much to build now had to be maintained at enormous cost by a family whose financial resources were strained to the limit, sinking under the combined weight of loss of rental income and exorbitant personal expenditure. The Charlemonts, too, were suffering badly from the loss of rental income. The Armagh estates, left to Lady Charlemont on the death of her husband, were now covered a fraction of the area they had when the earl died, being worth around £700 per year.[20]

On the whole, Sir Walter's finances were in a much better condition than those of any of his neighbours. His position as vice-president of the Court of Appeal in Cairo had previously provided him with a substantial income and, presumably, a healthy pension. He also had his inheritance as the heir of Drumsill House and now there was the legacy from his uncle. On his death Captain Shelton had left, in addition to his estates in Armagh, Down and Wiltshire, a sum of £5,000 charged on the Louth Hall Estates and a further £7,000 upon trust to be invested at the discretion of his trustees.[21] When

Captain Shelton died, his total estate had been valued at £135,329 10s. 2d.[22] Sir Walter's own portfolio of personal investments consisted, to a certain degree, of foreign bonds issued by companies such as the Lake Superior Paper Company, Sao Paulo Electric or Societe Frigorifique d'Egypt. He also invested £2,000 in 5 per cent War Loan stock. In 1918, for the purpose of super tax returns, Orr put Sir Walter's personal income for the previous year at £1,876 and that on Captain Shelton's estate at £4,891.[23]

Although Sir Walter seems to have had a substantial amount of money either invested in bonds and stocks or tied up in loans to less fortunate landlords, things were not all easy. On top of the fact that the income from rentals was becoming increasingly reduced, Sir Walter was now being faced with a problem that was to bring the ultimate downfall of many landed families throughout the British Isles – the dramatic rise in taxation and death duties. Estate duty had been introduced in 1894 at a rate ranging from 3 to 8 per cent depending on the size of the estate. By 1919 the rate had increased to 7 per cent for the smaller estates and 28 per cent on estates valued at over £1 million.[24] In November 1916, Sir Walter had to consider how to pay the duty on his new inheritance, due for payment in March of the following year. Orr suggested that he sold his Consols when the time came, although this in itself was a cause of concern 'as prices are nowadays so liable to fluctuate'.[25] The total estate duty on The Argory, Derrygally and the Water Eaton and Westmeath estates was assessed at £4,318, the Armagh estates not being included in this figure as they were pending sale in the Land Commission. Sir Walter finally decided to pay the amount in sixteen half-yearly instalments which, with the addition of interest at 3 per cent on the outstanding amount, would involve payments of around £600 per year for eight years. On top of this was the payment of succession duty, the annual instalments of which amounted to £44 19s. 11d. on Water Eaton, £91 11s. 7d. on the Argory and Derrygalley, and £51 1s. 4d. on the Armagh estate – a total of £187 12s. 10d. for which he was personally responsible.[26]

In addition to these payments, Sir Walter spent the first few years at The Argory making some necessary improvements to drainage, the water supply and the lighting in the form of a new acetylene gas plant. Out buildings had to be re-roofed and several structural alterations carried out. In total, Sir Walter calculated that he had spent nearly £2,500 on these essential details.[27] All in all, his new property was costing him dear at this stage and he, like many landlords, was beginning to question the value of his position. Sir Walter had no love of Ireland or, for that matter, of The Argory. In fact, by 1920 he was looking for ways round the clause in Captain Shelton's will which stipulated that the heir to the estate would have to make it his home, seeking to either sell or lease it.

In a letter to Orr,[28] while acknowledging the fact that his uncle would have wanted The Argory to remain in the family, Sir Walter used the current political instability as an argument to sell. Captain Shelton, he explained, 'certainly said to me at the time of the Ulster Volunteers that it would be impossible to live in Ireland once home rule had been granted.' He much preferred living in France, his health being given as his main reason. Again to Orr he argued that 'The Argory is not a desirable residence for me on account of the excessive dampness of the valley of the Black-water. I have, as you know, been advised by high medical authority to avoid a damp climate'.[29] Lady Bond had no great attachment to The Argory either. Sir Walter's one-time idea of putting central heating into the house were dismissed out of hand: 'Personally,' she wrote in her diary, 'it seems to me inappropriate to spend large sums of money on a house in *Ireland*'.[30] In the end they kept The Argory but, like an increasing number of other Irish landlords, spent less and less of their time in residence there.

As far as the rest of his inheritance went, Sir Walter quickly set about the process of retrenchment, selling one by one the estates that had been acquired by the MacGeough Bond family over centuries by one means or another. One of his first concerns was the sale of Drumsill House, there being none of the family left to live there now. Orr advised him to let the house go up for auction, estimating that it would sell for around £3,500. The 100 acres that remained would, he reckoned, bring in another £3,000.[31] In October 1916 the property was auctioned in four lots, the house itself being sold to the Revd Mr Millar for the expected amount of £3,500.[32] The rest of the land at Drumsill, approximately 75 acres, was auctioned off in September 1917.[33]

The next pressing concern was the sale of the estates. Captain Shelton's Armagh estate was already pending sale under the Wyndham act, the purchase money agreed at around £19,000. In addition to this sum, Orr explained that there would be a 12 per cent bonus which would be invested by Captain Shelton's trustees, but the interest of which would go directly to Sir Walter to use as he wished.[34] By June 1918 Orr was advising the sale of the Water Eaton estate in England, on the basis that after deductions it was now only bringing in about £800 per year. If sold at, say, £20,000, argued Orr, the money, if invested, would probably bring in more than that, without any of the problems of owning land:

> if you can sell land at a fair price now it would be better to get rid of it, as it seems to me that probably there will be increased taxation on the land in future and that persons who simply receive rents out of it will be heavily hit.[35]

The estate was valued at a sum of £21,621 and, on 17 September, Sir Walter received a letter from Orr informing him that the tenants had agreed to pay £20,500, a figure that he felt should be accepted. By April of the following year the deal was closed and the proceeds to be invested:

I have accordingly closed the sale [Water Eaton] this afternoon and shall see to the investment of the money tomorrow. The trustees all approve of investing in National War Bonds and … we [will] take up £5,000 of each of the 4 sets of Bonds … and that the balance after paying … costs of sale … should be invested in 5 per cent War Stock.[36]

By February 1921, the Westmeath estate was finally sold, £6,000 being advanced in cash, and the rest to be paid by the tenants.[37]

For the time being the MacGeough Bonds were in a similar position to many Irish landlords, having accumulated a sizeable amount of capital from the sale of their estates. Although a varying proportion of this capital went directly to mortgagees for the payment of other debts incurred by either the landlords themselves or their ancestors, most still had a healthy sum left after any outstanding payments were made.[38] While there were those like Harry Verner who spent with no thought for tomorrow, the majority of Irish landlords saw the need to invest their capital and live off the interest. For those who chose to invest there was a wide variety of investment opportunities available either in stocks and bonds or by buying shares in the multitude of companies expanding throughout the world, especially in the colonies and the Americas. Sir Walter chose to invest the proceeds from the sale of his estates in government stock and war bonds which, if unexciting, at least had the virtue of being safe.[39] Others were less fortunate, having been tempted by the prospect of a larger return to invest their capital in a more speculative way.

The great depression of the late twenties and early thirties saw the value being wiped off a multitude of investments. As share prices plummeted, the shock waves swept round the western world. In Ireland, as in the rest of the British Isles, many of the great landowners who had sold off their land and invested the proceeds in the stock market were to witness the loss of the bulk of their capital. For a significant number of them the stock market crash was the final blow as there was now nothing left for them to live on, there being no land left to generate any income. There were those who survived, however. Investors such as Sir Walter were to a certain degree protected from the worst of the disaster thanks to their innate caution. Having largely invested in relatively safe government stocks and bonds, their investments managed to hold some of their value.

This was not to be the end of the financial troubles for the owners of Ulster's big houses. In the 1930s The Argory, like so many houses throughout Ireland, was hit by a dramatic increase in the rates which were demanded. In the Armagh area many of the landed families which had managed to survive the storms of land agitation and rent strikes, war and economic ruin, now faced impossible rent demands for houses which were in some cases in a state of disrepair. Tynan Abbey, for example, was for the most part empty, Captain Stronge only occupying a small corner of the building. Parts of the house were uninhabitable due to the combination of damp in the basement and a leaking roof. In an appeal against the almost doubled valuation, the agent, Major Boyle, declared that it was even impossible to raise money by letting the property as a venue for country sports as you could no longer walk across the border to shoot in nearby Co. Monaghan. At The Argory the house, farm buildings, steward's house and cottages had previously had a rateable value of £83 5s. 0d. Under the revised valuation the rate was to be £165 10s. 0d., double the amount they had been paying.[40] Although many landlords appealed against these increases and had them reduced to a slightly more realistic figure, the combination of increased maintenance costs, increased rates and the constant battle against damp and decay led many landlords to question the value of their 'white elephants'.[41]

There were other factors that made the position of any remaining landed gentry in the area a difficult one. Many landlords who had weathered the storm of the land agitation and who had remained financially viable despite the sale of their land were finally crushed by the fear of intimidation and attack during the turbulent years during and following the partition of the country. Landlords in some southern counties were particularly badly affected by the guerrilla war that had broken out between the Irish Republican Army and the military following the success of Sinn Féin in the 1918 election. As the country degenerated into a state of lawlessness, the big houses became increasingly vulnerable. Many were raided for guns, while others were just attacked because they were perceived as representative of the British presence in Ireland. Bence-Jones estimates that around 200 of Ireland's big houses were lost in these years.[42]

Although the 'troubles' as they became known initially developed in the south, by the end of 1920 the unrest had spread well into Ulster. Fighting in the south was brought to an end in July 1921 with the signing of the treaty in which the British conceded dominion status to the 26 counties. Civil war followed, however, bringing another two years of atrocities, reprisals, and the further burning of big houses. Meanwhile the Government of Ireland Act of 1920 had brought about the existence of the separate state of Northern Ireland. The violence there was to continue unabated with sectarian fighting, IRA attacks and military reprisals becoming commonplace events in the years following partition.[43] Rural communities, and isolated country homes in particular, were easy targets for acts of terror and the big houses of Armagh and Tyrone were no exception. Of the houses close to The Argory, Charlemont Fort was the first to suffer this fate. Although no longer inhabited by Lady Charlemont, who had chosen to move to England, it did contain many of her fine furnishings, paintings and family records. The Mooney family now lived in part of the fort and acted as caretakers. On the night of 30 July 1920 the fort was broken into by members of the IRA who ordered the Mooneys to get out at once. They then dowsed the building in petrol and set it on fire, leaving it to burn to the ground.[44]

The threatening presence of the IRA in Co. Armagh was felt at The Argory, too. On 5 January 1923 Sir Walter received a letter from his agent in Armagh, Major Boyle enclosing the following notice received by himself and the land steward, Kinloch:

> Sir,
> I see by order of you that the lands of the Argory Demesne and Derry-galley Farm are poisoned. Take notice that if any dogs are poisoned on these lands, you are a doomed man, and shall be shot forthwith.
>
> And take further notice, that you must have all poison notices taken down before Thursday next 23 inst. or our threat will be put into force both on the landsteward and yourself.
>
> Remember this country is not the same as when you were Agent for Roxborough, we have lots of gunmen everywhere ready to carry out a job of this kind. And take further notice, that if one single dog is poisoned the houses of both the Argory and Derrygalley shall go up in the air. Pay attention to this, as your life is no more in our eyes than that of a dog. By Order. I.R.A.[45]

Despite his repeated assurances that his absence from Ireland at this time was for the good of his health, there can be no doubt that for Sir Walter, as for so many Irish gentry, the on-going threat of republican acts of terror deterred him from living at home. Well could his solicitor write, 'We are hoping for the best but things seem to be going from bad to worse in this country.'[46]

Living increasingly in London or at health spas on the continent, Sir Walter's and Lady Ada's visits to The Argory became fewer and shorter. Although the house and gardens were well tended and maintained, the household was now a mere shadow of what it had been in better times. There would be no room whatsoever for needless expense. In one of his many letters to the steward, Kinloch, Sir Walter wrote:

> I am much surprised that you sent for Mrs O'Brien to 'prepare' duck & chicken which you sent over, as I had *told* you that you were not to send for her … For looking after unoccupied house there are, besides 1) yourself, 2) John Garland, 3) Lizzie Conlan, 4) Stratton 5) Chauffeur Hamilton. Between five of you, you must manage without Anne O'Brien to pluck chicken.[47]

With the number of servants now reduced to single figures, The Argory had ceased to be the source of employment and centre of the community that it had been in Captain Shelton's time. Now it was little more than a large, empty house, occupied for most of the year by a handful of servants, shorn of both its land and the social prestige it had always represented.

Eventually Sir Walter took the decision to hand the property over to his son, Neville. In 1925 he wrote to Orr explaining that he had

> for some time been contemplating the assignment of my life interest in the annual income derived from Captain Shelton's Estate subject to the payment of a small annuity … My age and health will no longer allow me to bear the burden – especially as regards the house. For outside matters the work is now simple, being able to act on my own initiative; for inside matters I must try and work with Lady Bond which is difficult as managing is not one of her gifts. My idea is to put her and Tommy in the position they will occupy on my death …[48]

Finally in 1943, two years before his death, Sir Walter signed a deed of appointment handing over everything to his son.[49] On 21 November 1945, Sir Walter died at the age of 88.[50] Only days later his steward of 20 years, William Graham, followed him to the grave.[51]

Conclusion

The last of his line, Neville MacGeough Bond was to live on at The Argory, alone apart from a few servants, for another 30 years. He, like so many survivors of the great ascendancy, was seen as an isolated and rather eccentric addition to the local community. On a Sunday he would continue the tradition of Captain Shelton and Sir Walter by worshipping in St James' Church of Ireland, Moy. However he always made a point of first ascertaining the temperature of the church, and was rarely seen without layers of warm coats. In later years he spent his winters in Jamaica, the cold, damp air that creeps up from the Blackwater in winter making The Argory an uncomfortable place for one who, like his parents, needed the warmth of the sun. For the last decade of his life his only companion at The Argory was his housekeeper and good friend, Isobel Wright who, with her husband, visited him daily to ensure that he had a meal and to provide him with the company that he valued so much.

Of the landed gentry that had formed the social circle in this part of Armagh, he was one of the remaining few. Of the big houses described at the beginning of this work, The Argory was the only one to survive. The rest either disintegrated slowly into ruin or, as had so many in the southern counties, suffered a violent end, burning red against a night sky. After 1923 the Free State had become relatively peaceful, allowing those who remained to carry on in their own albeit increasingly isolated and impoverished way. Landlords in Northern Ireland, however, continued to be targets of IRA terrorism.

Many years earlier, in April 1923, Lady Ada MacGeough Bond had recorded in her diary, 'Motored to Tynan Abbey to lunch twice … The Norman Stronges and baby were there. Lady S. took me to see the garden. It's a charming place'.[1] Sixty years later, on the night of 21 January 1983, members of the provisional IRA broke their way into Tynan Abbey. Sir Norman, now eighty-six years of age, and his only son James were asleep in the house at the time. Both were dragged from their beds and shot dead. The intruders then set fire to the building, leaving it burning as they disappeared into the night. The ruins of Tynan Abbey remained standing until November 1998 when it was felt necessary, for safety reasons, to demolish them.[2]

The brutal murder of a close friend, one who lived in a similar situation to himself, was a dreadful shock for Mr Bond who had, himself, come face to face with terrorism just a few years earlier. A local man, Eric Lutton, often

6 Neville MacGeough Bond
(photo courtesy of
National Trust)

drove Mr Bond's car for him when he needed to travel anywhere. On the night of 1 May 1979 as he was taking Mr Bond to Portadown, members of the IRA ambushed them in the Argory grounds. Mr Lutton was shot dead and Mr Bond threatened. A bullet was fired in his direction, embedding itself in the door of the car beside him.[3] For many landlords throughout Ireland similar encounters with terror were the last straw, driving them forever from their houses. Mr Bond, shocked and dismayed by the events of that night, remained in his hotel suite for many months rather than return to live alone at The Argory. Eventually, however, he decided to return home to the house he loved.

Drumsill House, the original MacGeough Bond home but long since used as a hotel, also met its end at the hands of terrorists. On the night of Tuesday 11 October 1972 members of the IRA left a suitcase containing 50lb of explosives on the ground floor beside the kitchens. The explosion destroyed the building – the reason given was that it was 'being used as a place of entertainment by the security forces'.[4]

Other houses, having escaped the effects of terrorism, declined rapidly due to neglect and lack of money. The Charlemonts' mansion, Roxborough, was still being maintained at the turn of the century. In February 1899, the house saw what was probably its final social event in the form of a three-day-long hare-coursing meeting which was held in the grounds.[5] Even at this stage, however, the house had sadly deteriorated. According to Sean Barden,

> The estate, was now divided and mortgaged and Roxboro all but empty ... In a few years the neglected Roxboro would be less than adequate for any such assembly. In just thirty months from the gathering described

above, Charters wrote despondently, 'The ceiling of the Saloon has
fallen down and the wallpaper hanging down as well as the floor
which has risen, the whole place will shortly be a ruin'.[6]

These words were indeed prophetic. Within two decades the house had
fallen into complete ruin, used by local people as a source of building material.
Today the visitor to Moy, attracted by the massive wrought iron gates that
once guarded the main entrance to the castle, is disappointed to find that
they now lead to a modern bungalow and a large, empty field.

Churchill fared no better. Harry fulfilled his own prophesy and died
young, leaving the house and what remained of his estate to a lady friend
who, it is said, allowed herself to be cheated out of her complete inheritance.
Thus a proud and wealthy family of landowners and public representatives
died out in poverty and ignominy, victims of the combined effects of loss of
land and position and the degeneration of the family line. The house, now
abandoned, was finally pulled down in the 1920s. Today a few scattered
parkland trees and some cut stones half-buried in a field provide the only
hint that here once stood one of Co. Armagh's big houses and the home of
one of its principal families.

What of The Argory? Aware of the fact that he was the last in line and
concerned as to the fate of the property after his death, Neville offered it to
his cousin, Robert Smith, then living in England. Mr Smith, understandably,
felt that the cost involved in maintaining this property would be too great
and declined to take it on. Neville, increasingly worried that when he died
the house would, like Drumsill, be sold as a hotel or a nursing home, finally
took the advice of a close friend and approached the National Trust.[7] This
organisation would, he felt, have the expertise and resources necessary for
the maintenance of the house. The decision must have been a difficult one
but for Neville, like his great-uncle Ralph Shelton, the continued welfare of
the house he loved was his first concern. In 1979, after much negotiation, he
handed over the house and demesne along with a substantial sum of money
to the National Trust. The Northern Ireland government provided a grant to
enable necessary repairs to be carried out as well as giving an endowment
out of the Ulster Land Fund.[8] Neville carried on living in a small flat in the
north wing until his death in 1986 and was finally buried, according to his
wishes, in a consecrated plot in the garden.

Today the house still stands, perfectly preserved and full of the atmosphere of Edwardian Anglo-Ireland – a tribute not only to the ongoing work
of conservation being carried out by the National Trust, but also to the
determination of successive generations of MacGeough Bonds that The
Argory would be preserved intact. Land wars, social and political upheaval,
the degeneration of family lines and financial ruin brought about the

destruction of big house society in this part of Ulster, as it did throughout Ireland. The countryside round the sleepy village of Moy now contains only hints that once it was populated with the mansions of the great and powerful. Most of the mansions and all the titled families have long faded into history. In common with many parts of Ulster, however, the big houses of the minor gentry have fared much better, The Argory being a classic example.

The MacGeough Bonds were, like most of Ulster's minor gentry families, faced with the same challenges as their grander neighbours. They experienced the loss of rental income and the sale of their lands, they were subject to heavy taxation and death duties and they experienced the fear of intimidation and attack. However their inherent caution, especially when it came to financial matters and the fact that they were not totally dependent on Irish land for their income shielded them from the full impact of the land wars and successive land acts. Sir Walter's cautious investment of the proceeds from the sale of their estates meant that they were protected from the worst of the stock market crash that finally ruined so many. Their moderate lifestyle combined with Captain Shelton's determination to keep the house in the family and Neville's gift of the property to those best able to care for it, have left the house and demesne as a fitting memorial to a class of people and a way of life now gone.

In the end, as with so many in this ever-decreasing social circle, the family line has died out, the MacGeough Bonds passing into oblivion, their name now just a part of the history of this area. Unlike their neighbours, however, their house stands today exactly as it did at the height of its glory. On a sunny spring afternoon The Argory continues to gaze serenely down on the still depths of the Blackwater.

Notes

ABBREVIATION

PRONI   Public Record Office of Northern Ireland, Belfast

INTRODUCTION

1 M. Bence-Jones, *A guide to Irish country houses* (London, 1988), p. 279.
2 A. Day and P. McWilliams (eds) *Ordnance Survey memoirs of Ireland. Vol. I: County Armagh* (Belfast,1990), p. 127.
3 C.E.B. Brett, *Buildings of County Armagh* (Belfast, 1999), p. 100.
4 Ibid., p. 106
5 Ibid., p. 91.
6 Bence-Jones, *Guide*, p. 143.
7 Ibid., p. 249.
8 Ibid., p. 66.
9 D. Dunlop, *A memoir of the professional life of William J Barre esq., Member of the Royal Institute of Architects* (Belfast, 1868), photographic appendix.
10 Day, O.S. *memoirs*, p. 55.
11 J. Kerr, 'Churchill – home of the Verners', *Review: Journal of the Craigavon Historical Society*, 6:3.
12 Day, *O.S. memoirs*, p. 24.
13 P.O. Marlow, *The Argory* (London, 1992), p. 5.
14 Statistics from J. Bateman, *Great landowners of Great Britain and Ireland* (London, 1883).
15 Quoted in G. Jackson-Stops, 'The Argory, County Armagh 1', *Country Life*, 30 June 1983, p. 1768.
16 Marlow, *The Argory*, p. 27.
17 T.W. Moody, 'Fenianism, Home Rule and the land war', *in* T.W. Moody and F.X.Martin (eds) *The course of Irish history*, (Dublin,1994).
18 J.E., Pomfret, *The struggle for land in Ireland* (Princeton, 1930), p. xi.
19 M. Bence-Jones, *Twilight of the Ascendancy* (London, 1987).
20 T. Dooley, *The decline of the Big House in Ireland* (Dublin, 2002).
21 R.W. Kirkpatrick, 'Origins and development of the Land War in mid-Ulster, 1879–85' in F.S.L. Lyons and R.A.J. Hawkins (eds), *Ireland Under the Union: Varieties of Tension*, (Oxford, 1980).
22 Quoted in Kirkpatrick, 'Land War', p. 202.

1. THE ARGORY IN 1880

1 J. Lennox Kerr, *The unfortunate ship: the story of H.M. Troopship Birkenhead* (London, 1960), p. 49.
2 Ibid., p. 115.
3 'Birkenhead Survivors' Testimonies'. http://www.palmiped.btinternet.co.uk /BondShelton.htm
4 Cutting from *Belfast News Letter*, undated, among Argory papers.
5 *Irish Weekly Telegraph*, 9 Mar. 1916.
6 *Return of owners of land in cities and counties of towns in Ireland*, [C 1492], HC 1876, lxxx, 61.
7 *Griffith's Valuation*.
8 A.P. O'Dalaigh, 'The Moy Castle or Roxborough House', *Duiche Neill: Journal of The O Neill Country Historical Society* 7 (1992), p. 24.
9 *Tyrone Courier*, 7 July 1960.
10 Estate Diary, 1891, Argory papers.
11 Box A, Argory papers.
12 Captain Shelton's diary, 1898, Argory papers.
13 Argory papers.
14 PRONI, D/288/G/3.
15 Dooley, *Decline*, p. 55.
16 Shelton's diary, 1889, Argory papers.

17 Shelton's diaries, 1886–91, Argory papers.
18 E. Somerville, *Irish memoirs* (London, 1914), p. 71.
19 R.M. Young, *Belfast and the province of Ulster in the twentieth century* (Brighton, 1909), p. 308.
20 Dooley, *Decline*, p. 68.
21 Register of births, deaths and marriages, parish records, St James' Church of Ireland, Moy.
22 Shelton's diaries 1889–95, Argory Papers.
23 Bence-Jones, *Twilight*, p. 54.
24 B.M. Walker, *Ulster politics: the formative years, 1868–86* (Belfast, 1989), p. 3.
25 Young, *Belfast and the province of Ulster*, pp. 419 and 326.
26 National Archives of Ireland, T/8626.
27 Dooley, *Decline*, p. 81.
28 M. Craig, *The Volunteer earl* (London, 1948), pp. 140–1.
29 M. Egremont, *Balfour* (London, 1980), p. 110.
30 A.P.W. Malcolmson, PRONI, Introduction to D/288.

2. CHALLENGE TO THE LANDED INTEREST

1 W.E. Vaughan, *Landlords and tenants in mid-Victorian Ireland* (Oxford, 1996), p. 28.
2 PRONI, D/288/G/3.
3 Wann to Farrer, Orney & Co., PRONI, D/1606/5/5.
4 PRONI, D/236/488/1.
5 J.S. Donnelly Jr., *Landlord and tenant in nineteenth century Ireland* (Dublin, 1973).
6 J. Bardon, *A history of Ulster* (Belfast, 1992), p. 320.
7 R.V. Comerford, 'The land war and the politics of distress, 1877–82' in W.E. Vaughan (ed.), *A new history of Ireland: vi Ireland under the union ii, 1870–1921* (Oxford, 1996), p. 28.
8 Bardon, *History of Ulster*, p. 368.
9 Lord Charlemont to Boyle, 13 June 1879, PRONI, D/266/367/11/B.
10 Crossle to Sir William, 25 Nov. 1880, PRONI, D/236/488/1.
11 Crossle to Jackson and Prince, 24 Sept. 1880, PRONI, D/236/488/1.
12 Wann to Graves, 5 Jan. 1881, PRONI, D/236/488/1.
13 Crossle to Jackson, 25 Nov. 1880, Ibid.
14 Ibid., 7 Jan 1881.
15 Wann to Fyffe, 27 Jan 1881, PRONI, D/1606/1/2/B/51.
16 Dooley, *Decline*, p. 95.
17 Crossle to Sir William, 22 Oct. 1881, PRONI, D/236/488/1.
18 Crossle to Lady Verner, 22 May 1882, PRONI, D/236/488/2.
19 Quoted in Dooley, *Decline*, p. 101.
20 Crossle to Sir William, 8 Nov. 1881, PRONI, D/236/488/2.
21 Crossle to Lady Verner, 9 Sept. 1882, PRONI, D/236/488/3.
22 C.E.B. Brett, *Buildings of County Antrim* (Belfast, 1996), p. 72.
23 Ibid., p. 104.
24 Anne MacGeough Bond, will and probate, National Archives of Ireland, T/8626.
25 PRONI, D/288/F/31/10/52.
26 PRONI, D/288/G/3.
27 Box A, Argory papers.
28 Debrett, *Illustrated baronetage* (London, 1953), p. 840.
29 Walker *Ulster politics*, p. 159.
30 Ibid., p. 129.
31 Dooley, *Decline*, p. 211.
32 Sir Walter's diary, 27 Sept. 1883, Argory papers.
33 Dooley, *Decline*, p. 211.
34 B. Walker, 'Land question and elections in Ulster', in S. Clark, and J.S. Donnelly Jr. (eds), *Irish peasants: violence and political unrest 1780–1914*, eds. (Manchester, 1983), p. 259.
35 *Daily Mail*, 10 March 1916.
36 Bardon, *History of Ulster*, p. 440.
37 Walker, 'Land question,' p. 235.

3. CHANGED TIMES AT THE ARGORY 1916

1 *Armagh Guardian*, 17 March 1916.
2 Ibid.
3 Captain Shelton, second codicil to will, PRONI, D/288/C/2/29.
4 *Ulster Gazette*, 22 Nov 1945
5 Sir Walter's diary, 21 Feb 1917, Argory papers.

6 Lady Ada to Sir Walter, 22 Feb 1916, Argory papers.
7 Bence-Jones, *Twilight*, p.168.
8 Sir Walter's diary, 29 August 1917, Argory papers.
9 Lady Ada to Sir Walter, 15 May 1916, Argory papers.
10 F.S.L. Lyons, *Ireland since the Famine* (London, 1971), p. 398.
11 B.L. Solow, *The land question and the Irish economy* (Cambridge, 1971), p. 189.
12 T.W. Moody, 'Fenianism, Home Rule and the Land War', p. 289.
13 Bence-Jones, *Twilight*, p. 92.
14 Verner papers, PRONI, D/236/488.
15 *Return of Advances under the Purchase of Land (Ireland) Act, 1891, Section-thirty-three, in 1899–1900*, HC 1901, lxi and 1902, lxxxiv; and *Return of advances made under the Irish Land Act 1903 and Irish Land Act 1909*, HC 1914–16, liii.
16 Bence-Jones, *Twilight*.
17 Kerr, 'Churchill', p. 5.
18 Loose receipts, Argory papers.
19 Kerr, 'Churchill', p. 5.
20 S. Barden, *The last countess* (Belfast, 2002), p. 103.
21 Copy of will, PRONI, D/288/F/31/10/49.
22 Index of Wills 1916, PRONI.
23 Orr to MacGeough Bond, 10 Sept. 1918, PRONI, D/288/F/31/3.
24 Dooley, *Decline*, p. 136.
25 Orr to MacGeough Bond, 27 Nov. 1916, PRONI, D/288/F/31/1.
26 Ibid., 6 Feb 1918, PRONI, D/288/F/31/3.
27 MacGeough Bond to Orr, 11 Oct. 1920, PRONI, D/288/F/31/5.
28 Ibid., 29 Sept. 1920, PRONI, D/288/F/31/5.
29 Ibid.
30 Lady Ada's diary, 16 April 1923, Argory papers.
31 Orr to MacGeough Bond, 8 Sept. 1916, PRONI, D/288/F/31/1.
32 Ibid., 16 Oct 1916, PRONI, D/288/F/31/1.

33 Ibid., 14 Sept 1916, PRONI, D/288/F/31/1.
34 Ibid., 12 Feb. 1918, PRONI, D/288/F/31/3.
35 Ibid., 19 Jun 1918, PRONI, D/288/F/31/3.
36 Ibid., 7 April 1919, PRONI, D/288/F/31/7.
37 Irish Land Commission to MacGeough Bond, 3 Feb 1921, PRONI, D/288/F/31/9.
38 Dooley, *Decline*, p. 120.
39 Orr to MacGeough Bond, 7 April 1919, PRONI, D/288/F/31/7.
40 *Armagh Guardian*, 7 Feb. 1936.
41 Ibid.
42 Bence-Jones, *Twilight*, p.202.
43 Bardon, *History of Ulster*, pp. 484–95
44 Bardon, *The last countess*, p. 104.
45 Boyle to Sir Walter, 23 Jan. 1923, PRONI, D/288/F/31/10/30.
46 Corr to Sir Walter, 18 Jan. 1921, PRONI, D/288/F/31/9.
47 Sir Walter to Kinloch, 28 Jan. 1923, Letter Receipt Book, Argory papers.
48 Sir Walter to Orr, 24 Aug. 1925, ibid.
49 Copy of Sir Walter's Will, PRONI, D/288/C/2/38.
50 *Belfast News Letter*, 22 Nov. 1945.
51 *Tyrone Courier*, 29 Nov. 1945.

CONCLUSION

1 Lady Ada's diary, 23 April 1923, Argory papers.
2 Brett, *Buildings of County Armagh*, p. 88.
3 Personal interview, Mrs Isobel Wright, May 2003.
4 *Ulster Gazette*, 19 Oct 1972.
5 *Belfast News Letter*, 10 Feb 1899.
6 Barden, *The last countess*, p. 89.
7 Personal interview, Mrs Isobel Wright, May 2003.
8 G. Jackson-Stops, 'The Argory, Co. Armagh – II', *Country Life*, 7 July 1983, p. 20.